"It is not an overstatement to say that Jim Denison writes with the voice of a prophet, the insights of a cultural apologist, and the heart of a pastor. In *The Coming Tsunami*, Dr. Denison warns us of the tidal waves of ideologies that have rapidly caused our society to devolve and stripped us of biblical values. However, far from leaving us in despair, Denison provides us with the life raft of hope to survive. The bad news is that the tsunami is upon us; the good news is that it is possible for us to have gospel influence even in today's torrent of lies and deception if we stand on God's unwavering truth and his unending grace."

—**Chris Brooks, Senior Pastor of Woodside Bible Church and Host of *Equipped with Chris Brooks***

"Dr. Jim Denison invites us to engage our current cultural moment with urgency and consequence. His road map involves intellectual ferocity, cultural relevance, and compassionate generosity. We are five minutes until midnight. Engage."

—**Dr. Mac Pier, Founder, Movement.org; Co-Catalyst for Cities, Lausanne**

"In my work with Christ-following CEOs around the country, I've heard their growing concern about the challenges of being a Christian leader in America. Our moral compass as a nation is changing its true north. What was once perceived as true, even a decade ago, is being challenged and a new radically different cultural journey is being plotted. That's one reason I'm grateful for Jim Denison's new book, one I know will help all Christ-following leaders understand and better prepare for their leadership journey ahead—one where secularism might just become the dominant religion of our day."

—**Rick Lytle, President and CEO, CEO Forum, Inc.**

"This book is a clarion call for Christians who want to make a difference in a culture that may no longer want to hear our voice. *The Coming Tsunami* covers immense ground, but I especially appreciate Jim's chapter on the necessary medical ethics questions we should be asking of our 'post-truth' culture. If you want to learn how to live in this new world—but not be of this new world—read this book."

—Joel Allison, Former CEO of Baylor Scott & White Health

"We are presently enduring a cultural tidal wave crashing in on all fronts. For many of us in higher education, we realize the impact cultural shifts will have before reaching the shores of society at large. Dr. Jim Denison has helped us on numerous occasions carefully navigate the stormy cultural waters of our day. This book is an outstanding resource that will strengthen your faith, provide timely wisdom, and reveal incredible biblical insight for the challenges we face as Christians today."

—Adam C. Wright, Ph.D., President, Dallas Baptist University

"I can't imagine trying to navigate today's ideological tidal waves without this indispensable guide. In these pages, Denison captures the essence of every major cultural current and poses a thoughtful, redemptive response. He speaks truth without hate and offers correction without condemnation. Be assured our entire church staff will be given this seminal work as a must-read for facing an uncertain future with a certain faith."

—Howard K. Batson, Ph.D., Pastor, First Baptist Church of Amarillo

The Coming Tsunami

Why Christians Are Labeled Intolerant, Irrelevant, Oppressive, and Dangerous—and How We Can Turn the Tide

The Daily Article email newsletter is news discerned differently every Monday through Friday.
Subscribe for free at DenisonForum.org.

Biblical Insight to Tough Questions: Vols. 1–10

Between Compromise and Courage: The Choice Every Christian Must Make

Every Hour I Need Thee: A Practical Guide to Daily Prayer

Blessed: Eight Ways Christians Change Culture

To Follow in His Footsteps: A Daily Devotional through the Holy Sites of Israel

Bright Hope for Tomorrow: How Jesus' Parables Illuminate Our Darkest Days

Respectfully, I Disagree: How to Be a Civil Person in an Uncivil Time

The Greater Work: How Prayer Positions You to Receive All that Grace Intends to Give

How Does God See America?

Request these books at DenisonForum.org/store

The Coming Tsunami

Why Christians Are Labeled Intolerant, Irrelevant, Oppressive, and Dangerous—and How We Can Turn the Tide

Dr. Jim Denison

thecomingtsunami.com

Forefront
BOOKS

Contents

Foreword

A tsunami warning can be terrifying. An earthquake many miles away under the ocean sends a wall of water in your direction. You cannot stop it, but fortunately you can seek higher ground if you receive the warning in time.

Dr. Jim Denison warns us of a cultural tsunami brought about by four cultural earthquakes. The philosophy of postmodernism has created a post-truth culture where the truth becomes "your truth." The sexual revolution has changed sexual mores. Racial identity is forged through critical race theory and other associated isms and ideologies. Attacks on Christians are encouraged and celebrated as a secular religion grows stronger every day.

He wisely explains how these secular forces also show up in the desire to pass the misnamed Equality Act and how major businesses have become "woke." He even describes how these secular waves influence how we think about genetics and designer babies.

The response to a physical tsunami is to retreat to safer ground. Jim Denison is not calling for us to run away from these waves but to defend biblical truth, to defend biblical sexuality, to defend biblical equality, and to defend biblical Christians.

His book helps us diagnose the state of our culture by identifying these earthquakes. But it also offers a prescription of proactive, biblical steps to redeem the challenges we face today.

This is a book you need to buy, read, and apply immediately.

Kerby Anderson
President, Probe Ministries
Host, *Point of View* radio talk show

Warning signs

The interior of an office building shakes uncontrollably. A large swath of ceiling crumbles to the floor of an airport. Endless, surging waves shove two-ton cars as if they were toys. Rumbling debris flows through a wide city street.

Then the real terror begins.

People scramble to higher ground. Those already in a secure place hoist others up. The camera quickly pans left and reveals the imminent threat a few dozen feet beneath them: an ocean of surging water irrevocably changing their landscape.

To watch this footage of dual natural disasters compiled by National Geographic is to witness the raw, unpredictable, and tragic power of nature.

The details are just as staggering. On March 11, 2011, at 2:46 p.m. local time, an earthquake struck forty-five miles northeast of Japan.

Less than an hour later, the first of several tsunami waves hit Japan's coastline. They reached heights of up to 128 feet and traveled inland as far as six miles, flooding an area of approximately 217 square miles.

Nearly 16,000 people were killed. More than 120,000 buildings were destroyed; 726,000 others were damaged. The tsunami caused a cooling system failure at the Fukushima Daiichi Nuclear Power Plant. The total economic cost could reach $235 billion, making it the costliest natural disaster in world history.

The damage could have been even worse.

Tokyo residents received a minute of warning thanks to Japan's earthquake early-warning systems. The system stopped high-speed trains and factory assembly lines. People also received text alerts about the earthquake and tsunami warnings on their cellphones.

However, the Japan Meteorological Agency was criticized in the tsunami's aftermath for issuing an initial warning that underestimated the size of the wave. In some regions, only 58 percent of people headed for higher ground immediately after the earthquake.

In addition, officials had issued sixteen tsunami warnings in the previous four years, but many people experienced only small or negligible tsunamis. As a result, they became complacent; 10 percent of those interviewed after the tragedy did not think a tsunami would come at all.

This book is a warning sign.

I pray that the full brunt of the cultural tsunami I see coming fails to arrive. But I fear that the reverberations of past earthquakes have already arrived on our shores.

The tsunami is coming. Are you ready?

A lopsided conflict?

It is often said that America is caught in the throes of a culture war. However, in recent years, it's become a lopsided conflict at best.

Consider how Americans have changed their minds on the moral acceptability of these behaviors over the last twenty years:

- Same-sex relationships rose from 40 percent to 66 percent.

- Out-of-marriage childbirth rose from 59 percent to 66 percent.

- Sex between unmarried adults rose from 53 percent to 72 percent.

- Divorce rose from 59 percent to 77 percent.

As an evangelical Christian, I grieve each of these trends. I view these issues through a biblical lens and therefore believe that these behaviors are outside of God's will for us. But when people like me declare this truth in public, we are immediately dismissed as homophobic, bigoted, and even dangerous to society.

Unsurprisingly, 66 percent of white evangelical Protestants say their religious beliefs conflict with mainstream American culture; only 42 percent of all US adults feel the same way. And 77 percent of white evangelicals expect to lose influence under the Biden administration.

What is going on?

A threat we've never faced

Tsunamis are produced when earthquakes or volcanic eruptions far beneath the ocean's surface produce giant waves on that surface that devastate those in their path. In the same way, the moral and spiritual tsunamis we are experiencing have their origins in events and ideas that are less apparent to us.

These tidal waves are threatening to submerge evangelical Christians in America and the biblical morality we proclaim. But here's the good news: unlike tsunami's in nature, which cannot be stopped once they have been created, it's not too late to stop the moral tsunamis of our day.

If we will identify the four earthquakes that have created these tidal waves and recognize the enormous danger they represent, we can then take proactive, biblical steps to redeem these challenges as opportunities for God's word and grace.

But we must act now.

I believe evangelical Christians are facing a threat we have not faced before in American history. In fact, the more I have worked on this book, the more gravely concerned I have become. I know this sounds like hyperbole intended to sell books, but it's not. It's my heartfelt conviction based on the facts we will discuss throughout this book.

Defining "evangelicals"

Before I proceed, I need to clarify what I mean by "evangelicals." The term has become politicized and is often used in a highly pejorative way today. For my purposes, however, I am referring not to a political group but to those who espouse a specific set of beliefs.

In addition, I am referring to evangelicals in America. I recognize and celebrate the fact that evangelicals are found around the world. It has been my privilege to work personally with evangelicals in Cuba, China, Bangladesh, South America, and across Europe. However, their cultural issues are often different from those we face in the US.

For this reason, and because I have far less personal insight into challenges in other cultures, I am restricting my focus in this book to American evangelicals.

The National Association of Evangelicals (NAE) is one of the leading organizations for evangelicals in the US. It notes that the term *evangelical* comes from the Greek word *euangelion*, meaning the "good news" or the "gospel." Thus, evangelical faith focuses on the "good news" that salvation is available to lost people through faith in Jesus Christ.

The NAE cites a summary of evangelical distinctives first proposed by historian David Bebbington and now used widely:

- Conversionism: the belief that we need to be transformed through a "born-again" experience and a lifelong process of following Jesus as Lord

- Activism: expressing and demonstrating the gospel in missionary and social reform efforts

- Biblicism: a high regard for and obedience to Scripture as our ultimate authority

- Crucicentrism: a stress on the sacrifice of Jesus on the cross as making possible our redemption

In addition, evangelicals stand apart from the rest of society on a variety of moral issues:

- Of evangelicals, 32 percent say "religious belief is a matter of personal opinion [and] not about objective truth," in contrast to 60 percent of Americans who agree.

- Of white evangelicals, 67 percent would make abortion illegal except in cases of rape, incest, or threats to a mother's life; only 37 percent of all Americans agree.

- Of white evangelicals, 34 percent support same-sex marriage, in contrast to 70 percent of all Americans who agree.

In summary, when I speak of American "evangelicals," I am referring to people who believe the Bible is our ultimate authority, salvation is only through faith in Christ, non-Christians need to hear and accept the gospel, and the Bible forbids all sexual relationships outside of a monogamous marriage of one man and one woman.

While I consider these beliefs to be the orthodox, biblical positions of Christians for twenty centuries, those who embrace them today are increasingly marginalized and rejected by our secularized society. By contrast, those who identify as Christians but do not embrace these tenets are under far less attack today.

It's starting to rain

Before I proceed, let me offer some personal background.

My father was very active in his church until he fought in World War II and then never attended worship again. As a result, I grew up in a loving home but with no spiritual life and all my dad's questions: Why is there war? What about other religions? Why does God allow suffering? What about science and faith?

I was invited to church as a teenager and felt attracted to the faith of those I met there. At the age of fifteen, I prayed a salvation prayer and was baptized a few months later. However, my questions persisted. Encountering C. S. Lewis's *Mere Christianity* was transforming for me—for the first time, I met someone who grappled with intellectual questions as I did.

From that day to this, my calling has been to help people respond biblically and redemptively to the intellectual and cultural issues of our day. My life verse is Ephesians 4:12, "to equip the saints for the work of ministry." My mission is to help the church change the culture.

I earned a Ph.D. in philosophy of religion and apologetics and have taught in four seminaries in the areas of faith and culture. I pastored four churches with a combined membership of over twenty thousand; in each, my mission was to help our members use their influence to shape the culture. We founded Denison Forum, a nonprofit ministry that considers the day's news from a biblical perspective, in 2009 so I could devote full-time attention to this calling.

Over these decades, I have been following cultural developments with professional and personal passion. I say all of that to say this: I have never been as concerned about the trajectory of our culture as I am today. I have never been as convinced that evangelical Christians face unprecedented condemnation and opposition as I am today. And I have never been as burdened about the future of our nation and the threat of divine judgment as I am right now.

It feels as if I have been building an ark all my life, and now it is starting to rain.

Os Guinness notes:

> There are times when history and human decisions appear to meet in a single point to cast the die of a nation's fortunes—for Rome, Caesar's crossing the Rubicon; for England, Sir Francis Drake's defeat of the Spanish Armada; for the United States, the first shots fired at Lexington and Concord.
>
> There are other times when the fateful hinge is a period and not a day, when the accumulated consequences of an era stamp history as sharply as any date or event. So it was with the Civil War era; thus it was also with the Depression years.

We are living in such an era now. Whether the "fateful hinge" of history swings toward God's favor or his judgment is the pressing question of our day.

This book is intended to equip Christians to understand where we are, how we got here, and how we can respond redemptively. We'll identify the four specific threats we face, explore their consequences for evangelicals and our larger culture, and chart strategic and redemptive ways we can respond before it is too late.

In other words, four major earthquakes occurred in the last century that have shifted the ground beneath our feet. Whether you're aware of their occurrence or where they originated makes no difference. The coming cultural tsunami will greatly affect you as a Christian in the coming years—if it hasn't already. It will undoubtedly influence and affect your children and grandchildren.

But, as Christians, we are never without hope.

The Bible describes men from the tribe of Issachar "who had understanding of the times, to know what Israel ought to do" (1 Chronicles 12:32). Let's join their tribe, to the glory of God.

With God's help and by his grace, let's turn the tide of this tsunami before it overtakes us.

NOTE: This book is intended to be an introduction to the threats evangelicals are facing today. For updated responses to continuing news and issues, as well as practical steps for pastors, Christian leaders, churches, and ministries, I invite you to consult the companion website at thecomingtsunami.com.

PART 1

Four earthquakes

"Opinion has caused more trouble on this little earth than plagues or earthquakes."

— **VOLTAIRE**

As multiple earthquakes hundreds of miles away from any shore can result in a singular, sweeping tsunami that plunges a country's coastline into chaos, so too can long-past cultural upheavals threaten to drown Christianity. Though dozens of such quakes have occurred in the past, this book focuses on four in particular:

1. The rise of a "post-truth" culture

2. The rise of the sexual revolution

3. The rise of Critical Theory

4. The rise of secular religion

While each "quake" rightly deserves its own long-form treatment, I see the confluence of these events as the gravest threat that evangelical Christianity has ever faced in my lifetime. Taken together, the cultural acceptance of these four ideologies has seismically shifted our world. And I do not believe that their repercussions have yet to be fully experienced.

However, our calling as Christians is not to flee, even from imminent danger. Rather, we were given a mandate two thousand years ago to do just the opposite.

Every Christian's commission

One of my favorite places on earth is Caesarea Philippi. Situated twenty-five miles north of the Sea of Galilee at the base of Mount Hermon, the site is named for Philip II, the third son of Herod the Great, who made it his capital city following his famous father's death.

Whenever I lead study tours to Israel, we always make our way here. The location is stunning in its beauty: a massive cliff stands before us in which a large cave is situated. A torrent of water springs from the ground beneath the cave and forms a beautiful river. The entire area has been made into a park where families and school groups come to spend the day.

Despite its beauty, the area has long been associated with idolatry. Fourteen temples to the worship of Baal have been identified in the vicinity. Travelers carved niches in the cliff in which they placed their personal idols in the hopes that they would protect them.

In addition, Herod the Great built a marble temple in front of the cave to the worship of Augustus Caesar. Adjacent temples were constructed for Zeus and other gods of the Greek and Roman pantheon.

The site was especially used for the worship of the Greek god Pan, who was thought to have lived in the large cave located here. The area is therefore known today as *Banias*, the Arabic version of *Panias* (Arabic has no equivalent for the letter "p"). The worship of Pan involved forms of sexual immorality I will not describe here. Suffice it to say, absolutely horrific things happened in this place.

The cave where Pan was thought to have lived originally opened to a chasm through which the spring flowed. The ancient Jewish historian Josephus described it as "a horrible precipice, that descends abruptly to a vast depth: it contains a mighty quantity of water, which is immovable; and when anybody lets down anything to measure the depth of the earth beneath the water, no length of cord is sufficient to reach it." An earthquake in 1837 filled the cave and diverted the spring, which now emerges at its base.

Because this chasm was deeper than ancient people could measure, they thought of it as the gate or entrance to the underworld, or Hades, or "hell." As a result, an ancient inscription testifies to the cave and its immeasurable spring as the "gate of hell."

Standing here, confronting every kind of idolatry known to their day, Jesus asked his disciples, "Who do people say that the Son of Man is?" (Matthew 16:13). They told him that some thought him to be John the Baptist, Elijah, Jeremiah, or another prophet (v. 14). Then he asked them, "But who do you say that I am?" (v. 15).

Peter responded with his famous declaration, "You are the Christ, the Son of the living God" (v. 16). In return, Jesus announced, "On this rock I will build my church, and the gates of hell shall not prevail against it" (v. 18).

This was the first time Jesus used the word *church*. He founded his church, not at the temple in Jerusalem or the synagogue in Capernaum, but at Caesarea Philippi while standing before the gates of hell.

I am convinced that Jesus was pointing to that cave and the idolatrous immorality it represented when he said literally of his church, "And the gates of hell shall not withstand its assault."

From then until now, our commission has been to "assault the gates of hell," to "go therefore and make disciples of all nations" (Matthew 28:19), to be Jesus' witnesses "to the end of the earth" (Acts 1:8).

This commission to attack the gates of hell by sharing the good news of God's love has never been more urgent or dangerous for American Christians than it is today.

"We live in the postmodern world, where everything is possible and almost nothing is certain." —**VACLAV HAVEL**

1

The rise of a "post-truth" culture: Are evangelicals intolerant?

I remember vividly when I was caught in a riptide in the Gulf of Mexico.

Our family had come to the beach at Galveston for the day. I was in elementary school at the time. Despite my parents' warnings, I ventured out farther into the ocean than I should have. Before I knew it, an undercurrent had captured me and was sweeping me away from land. I tried to fight it, but the harder I swam, the farther I was carried from safety.

Then I remembered my mother's admonition: if you're caught in an undertow, don't try to swim against it. Instead, swim parallel to the beach. Eventually, you'll make your way out of the riptide to safety. That's what I did, finally getting back to land.

But I'll always remember the power of that unseen current.

Erwin Lutzer describes a "cultural current" as "a dominant idea promoted by the media and willingly adopted by a critical mass of people who want to believe a myth so badly they will close their minds to all contrary evidence." He warns: "When such a cultural movement gains momentum, people will stare at facts and filter out what they don't want to believe. Contrary evidence will be ignored or reinterpreted to fit their deepest wishes. And the more people who believe the myth, the more difficult it is for those who wish to counter it. In a spirit of euphoria, all warning signs are brushed aside. *Before we know it, we are in a world where facts do not matter.*"

We are in such a "cultural current" today.

The truth becomes *your* truth

The Christian movement was founded on the factual claim that Jesus of Nazareth is the Messiah, the Son of God, our Savior and Lord. He himself taught us that he is "the way, and the truth, and the life" (John 14:6). He assured his followers, "If you abide in my word, you are truly my disciples, and you will know the truth, and the truth will set you free" (John 8:31–32). Then Jesus proved the truth of his words by his miraculous deeds and, most of all, by his resurrection from the dead (cf. 1 Corinthians 15:19–20).

"Truth" for the first Christians was objective and based on the revelation of God through his word and his Son. The first generations of the Christian movement saw the church spreading throughout the Roman Empire and beyond to share this truth with the world. As Christianity moved beyond its Jewish roots, however, it began engaging with the secular, pagan world. In those days, centuries before a printed Bible, the question of truth arose again.

Over time, the church came to believe that its creeds, councils, and papal pronouncements were the authorities by which God's word was to be interpreted.

Fast-forward to the eighteenth century and the Enlightenment. German philosopher Immanuel Kant (1724–1804) spoke for many with his injunction, "Have courage to use your own reason!" Whether we are thinking of the Enlightenment in France, Scotland, Germany, Switzerland, England, or America, the common narrative was a call to question inherited beliefs and to seek progress through personal reason.

Kant's contributions to the nature of objective truth were especially significant. To summarize a very complex subject, he taught us that our minds interpret our senses, resulting in "knowledge." However, since your sensory experiences are different from mine and your mind interprets your senses in ways that are unique to you, there can be no such thing as "objective" truth. All truth claims by definition must be subjective and personal.

A secular utopia

Danish philosopher Søren Kierkegaard (1813–1855) believed that truth is chosen and acted upon. Faith is not mere intellectual assent but the total commitment of our lives to something or someone. Such commitment is by definition subjective since its results cannot be known before they are experienced. His passion for the individual's choice made Kierkegaard the "father of existentialism." The philosophy attributed to him stresses personal choice and identity as the basis for life.

German philosopher Friedrich Nietzsche (1844–1900) agreed with Kant that our language reflects not reality itself but our experience of it. For example, there is no such thing as "leaves," only individual "leafs" that we experience and synthesize into a universal concept. Nietzsche therefore claimed that language is purely individual and the imposition of our "will to power" on others. He was convinced that the "will to power" is the basic drive in human nature and urged us to assert our own "will" to become overcomers in the world.

Charles Sanders Peirce (1839–1914) further taught that truth is "opinion which is fated to be ultimately agreed to by all who investigate." What works for most people will be true, a philosophy known as "pragmatism."

These thinkers set the stage for what is now known as "postmodernism," the worldview that sees all truth claims as personal, individual, and subjective. Three men especially advanced this narrative and formed our culture's view of truth today.

- Michel Foucault (1926–84) agreed with Nietzsche that we must reject all claims to objective knowledge and instead focus on our personal experiences.

- Jacques Derrida (1930–2004) believed that we "create" our own world by speaking of it. He taught that language possesses no fixed meaning and is not connected to a fixed reality.

- Richard Rorty (1931–2007), one of America's most popular philosophers, taught that since no foundational truths exist apart from our ability to use words to describe them, "truth" is our description of the world in a way that works for us.

In Rorty's view, society must banish any attempts to require and enforce one particular view of reality and truth over another. In this way, we can build stronger communities in which people will be more tolerant of each other. His vision offers an enticing, accessible, and nonjudgmental alternative to the Christian worldview built upon a single Way, Truth, and Life (John 14:6).

However, as we will see later, to claim there is no such thing as absolute truth is to make an absolute truth claim. Those who reject objective ethics can claim no intrinsic ability to judge even the Holocaust or 9/11 since they were the expression of the "truths" of their perpetrators.

The media is driven by narrative, not news

When Prince Harry and Meghan announced that they would no longer deal with the UK's biggest tabloid newspapers, their statement made global headlines. Their decision came as no surprise, but their explanation is worth considering: "When power is enjoyed without responsibility, the trust we all place in this much-needed industry is degraded."

During the coronavirus pandemic, Gallup asked Americans to rate the way nine leaders and institutions are responding to the crisis. US hospitals came in first with an 88 percent approval rating. Dead last, at 44 percent, was the news media. This is not a new trend. Between 2003 and 2016, the percentage of Americans who said they trust the media fell from 53 percent to 32 percent.

America's founders understood the vital role a free press plays in strengthening democracy, which is why they made this freedom part of the First Amendment to the US Constitution. I remember a day when journalist Walter Cronkite was known as "the most trusted man in America" and the news media were valued for their objectivity.

What changed?

The *Columbia Journalism Review* reports that there has been a profound shift in news coverage from "who, what, when, and where" to "why." The writer thinks his colleagues should be more transparent about this shift: "It may be time for journalists to acknowledge that they write from a set of values, not simply from a disinterested effort at truth."

In a culture that rejects objective values and absolute truth claims, each person's opinion is their "truth," media included. As a result, it is now commonplace for media and platforms to report narratives more than news, interpreting events and seeking to persuade their audience to adopt their worldview. What was once the purview of the opinion pages and editorials is now the philosophy behind "news" reporting.

Social media platforms are increasingly aligned with the secular worldview of our day as well. As we will see in chapter 7, they illustrate a movement of businesses that promote LGBTQ agendas and other "woke" ideologies. It is therefore unsurprising that these platforms would censor content with which they disagree, including content from those who embrace biblical morality.

Rather than reporting the world objectively, the real business of media is business. They must know what constituents their advertisers seek to reach, then create content that appeals to these constituents. Since objectivity is impossible, subjectivity rules.

And "truth" loses.

The foundational quake

Apologist Mary Jo Sharp writes:

> We live in a time when it has become difficult to discuss belief in God in our society. Why? Many factors may contribute but a prominent reason is that our society has steadily grown more skeptical that such a thing as truth exists. Yet, in our daily conversations and lives, most people will not explicitly say, "I'm not sure that truth exists." The people we encounter more likely have been influenced by their culture much more subtly— even subconsciously—to believe that no one has

the truth. They will have a hard time articulating why they don't believe in truth or that they don't believe truth exists. Rather, they will use cultural catch phrases, "We should be tolerant;" "Don't be a hater;" "Everyone has their own way;" and "Who are you to judge?"

She is right: most Americans who deny the existence of truth can't explain or defend their denial. But this makes the consequences of our "post-truth" culture no less dangerous.

The postmodern denial of truth is the first earthquake contributing to the cultural tsunami against which biblical Christians are standing today. It is also foundational to all the others. To shift the analogy, it is the first layer of the cake many are consuming.

This rejection of objective truth undermines or denies every essential truth claim of the Christian faith:

- Jesus said to his Father, "Your word is truth" (John 17:17). However, this cannot be the case if there is no such thing as "truth." As a result, the Bible is merely a diary of religious experience rather than the authoritative word of God.

- Jesus said of himself, "I am the way, and the truth, and the life. No one comes to the Father except through me" (John 14:6). However, this cannot be true if "the" way, "the" truth, or "the" life do not exist. As a result, evangelism is the improper imposition of our personal truth on others.

- Peter proclaimed, "There is salvation in no one else, for there is no other name under heaven given among men by which we must be saved" (Acts 4:12). However, a postmodernist would reply that this was just his truth, not the truth, since we know that the truth does not exist.

- Jesus commissioned his followers to "make disciples of all nations" (Matthew 28:19). To a postmodernist, this is the improper imposition of our culture on other cultures.

As we will see, this denial of truth casts those who believe in biblical truth as outdated and irrelevant at best, if not dangerous to society and our best future.

And when arguments based on objective truth no longer have merit in the court of public opinion, who adjudicates sexuality and gender?

If the first quake of the rise of our post-truth culture was harder to detect, the second quake has made headlines for decades.

"Part of the sexual revolution is bringing rationality to sexuality. Because when you don't embrace sexuality in a normal way, you get the twisted kinds, and the kinds that destroy lives." —HUGH HEFNER

2

The rise of the sexual revolution: Are evangelicals irrelevant?

I am writing this book in June 2021. Since President Bill Clinton declared June "Gay & Lesbian Pride Month" in 1999, this has also been a month that celebrates LGBTQ people and ideology. As a measure of our society's evolution on this subject, we are seeing responses to "pride" that are unprecedented in our nation's history.

For example, Kellogg's cereal unveiled products celebrating the fact that "no matter who you are, who you love, or what pronouns you use, you're too awesome to fit into a (cereal) box." The children's cartoon *Rugrats* has been relaunched, this time with a lesbian single mom as one of the characters.

Not to be outdone, Nickelodeon released a video by its kids' program *Blue's Clues & You!* that takes place at a Pride parade. It is narrated by an animated version of drag performer and activist Nina West. The video includes families with two moms, two dads, trans-identified members, and "ace, bi and pan" parents. One of the characters displays scars from surgery used to change its gender from female to male. The narrator sings, "Love is love is love you see, and everyone should love proudly." West adds, "Allies to the queer community can love their friends so proudly."

Also in June 2021, the San Francisco Giants became the first Major League Baseball team to wear Pride uniforms. Their on-field caps featured the "SF" logo with colors depicting the Progress Pride Flag; each jersey had a patch on the right sleeve depicting the design.

These stories illustrate the second cultural earthquake that biblical Christians must understand before it changes the world our children and grandchildren will inhabit.

"The detrimental impact of sexual repression"

In *The Rise and Triumph of the Modern Self*, historian Carl Trueman explains our cultural march to sexual "freedom" with precision and clarity. He begins with writer Charles Taylor's concept of competing worldviews identified as *mimesis* and *poiesis*. The mimetic worldview considers the world to have meaning that humans must discover and live by. Poiesis, by contrast, believes the world to be "raw material" out of which individuals create meaning and purpose.

Trueman explains our progression from the mimetic to the poietic through the work of Philip Rieff, who traced culture from the political man (Greece), the religious man (Christianity), the economic man (Capitalism/Marx), and finally to the psychological man (Modern). We are now in the era of the psychological man with its quest for affirmation and commitment to "expressive individualism."

According to this worldview, it is left to each of us to discover and forge meaning in the world wherever and however we wish. We are like people standing before a Jackson Pollock painting seeking to connect its apparently random splotches into cohesive meaning for ourselves.

Jean-Jacques Rousseau was instrumental in this cultural trajectory with his argument that social structures create evils. The individual before society is basically good; morality would come easily to us if we were in nature. *Authenticity*, free from societal restraints, is the key to flourishing, or so Rousseau claimed. Romantic poets such as William Wordsworth, Percy Bysshe Shelley, and William Blake stirred the sentiments of their audiences and provoked emotivism that brought Rousseau's ideas to the masses.

As previously noted, Friedrich Nietzsche contributed to this narrative with his denial of objective meaning in language and his encouragement for us to overcome the power motives of others. Karl Marx added that human nature is always in flux because it is swayed by economic factors and is materialistically determined by them. Charles Darwin convinced us that we are essentially animals with no need (or capacity for) a higher explanation for life.

Sigmund Freud then provided the crucial link to the sexual revolution with his assertion that we are sexual beings at our core. He convinced many that sexual freedom and authenticity are vital to flourishing for individuals and society. His protégé Wilhelm Reich argued that sexual expression was natural and that the control of sexual energies by the family, institutionalized sexual morality, and the state were destructive. In his view, sexual repression profoundly distorted psychological development.

Jeffrey Escoffier writes:

> It is difficult to overestimate the impact of Wilhelm Reich's thinking about sexuality on intellectuals and more indirectly on the general

culture. The sexual revolution of the 1960s was initiated by people who shared many of Reich's beliefs (whether or not they got them from him directly) about the detrimental impact of sexual repression. Many of the first people on the barricades of the sexual revolution were inspired by Reich.

The fact that such a large-scale cultural phenomenon as the sexual revolution could be argued to have stemmed from the writings of a lesser-known philosopher is further proof that small tremors can cause grave, far-reaching, long-lasting consequences.

Four cultural factors

As these philosophical movements were gaining ground and coalescing, social and environmental factors were creating the context for them to take root in the larger culture. Millions of soldiers returned home from World War II to seek a new life for themselves. The GI Bill of Rights gave them money to attend college, purchase homes, and buy farms. They married and had families in the midst of the greatest economic boom in generations. However, the post-war era also provoked disruptive changes that created the climate for what became the sexual revolution of the 1960s. Four factors were especially significant.

One: The role of women

Nearly nineteen million American women held jobs during the war. Of those, around six million entered the labor force afterward. In addition, around 350,000 American women served in the military during the war. Many women who entered the workforce faced inequities of income and opportunity, sparking a drive for equal rights.

In 1960, the first birth control pill was approved by the Food and Drug Administration of the United States. For the first time, women were in charge of their fertility and could have sex without worrying about an unwanted pregnancy.

Helen Gurley Brown's book *Sex and the Single Girl* (1962) encouraged single women to be sexually active. Betty Friedan's book *The Feminine Mystique* (1963) argued that women are victims of a false belief system requiring them to find identity and meaning in their lives through their husbands and children.

Two: The growth of pornography

Hugh Hefner scandalized many when he began publishing *Playboy* magazine in 1953. In 1982, videotape moved films out of theaters and into private homes. In the late 1990s, pornographic films were distributed on DVD. Then the internet made pornography an epidemic available to every cellphone in America.

The courts struggled to keep up with this growing tide. In 1957's *Butler v. Michigan*, the Supreme Court rejected the principle that adult material must be restricted because it might harm minors. This ruling repudiated the earlier, longstanding test for obscenity that declared material obscene if it tended to "deprave and corrupt those whose minds are open to such immoral influences," including children.

In 1964's *Jacobellis v. Ohio*, the court struck down "community standards" for pornography, determining that such decisions were to be national rather than local. In 1969's *Stanley v. Georgia*, the court found that a state cannot prohibit citizens from possessing obscene material for personal use.

Three: The countercultural movement

The 1960s saw a rising movement protesting against the war in Vietnam and promoting rock music, the use of drugs, public displays of nudity, and complete freedom of sexual activity. "Make love, not war" became the slogan of an era. This movement made its way onto college campuses; by the end of the decade, colleges began relaxing their regulations, permitting coed dorms.

Four: Gay rights

The Stonewall Riots in 1969 were a galvanizing event in the movement for LGBTQ rights. Inspired by the civil rights struggles of the 1960s, this movement began working strategically to normalize LGBTQ people and behavior, legalize such behavior, and stigmatize those who disagree.

Normalizing began through popular media (the TV show *Will & Grace* is one example) and continues today through Pride Month and other efforts to make LGBTQ people and behavior ubiquitous and accepted. For example, GLAAD has been pressuring television producers to include more LGBTQ characters on broadcast and cable television; the number recently reached 10 percent, though the organization is pushing for 20 percent by 2025. (Note that the LGBTQ population of the US was 5.6 percent as of 2020.)

Normalizing led to legalizing same-sex relationships. In 2003's *Lawrence v. Texas*, the Supreme Court ruled that intimate consensual sexual conduct is protected by the Fourteenth Amendment, a ruling that struck down sodomy laws. In 2004, Massachusetts became the first US state to legalize same-sex marriage. In 2015's *Obergefell v. Hodges*, the Supreme Court ruled that states must license and recognize same-sex marriages.

Now we are in the era of stigmatizing those who disagree.

Christians who advocate for biblical morality are caricatured as homophobic, prejudiced, and discriminatory. We are viewed through the same lens with which racists are seen. As we will note in the next chapter, this perspective leads to the claim that Christians are oppressors of oppressed minorities. And as we will see in chapter 5, this perspective has led directly to the Equality Act and other attacks on religious freedom in America.

How the sexual revolution undermines Christianity

The sexual revolution that began in the 1960s and continues today undermines and opposes the Christian faith and witness in powerful ways.

First, it challenges biblical authority and relevance.

According to Scripture, God intends sex as a celebration of intimacy and the means of procreation for one man and one woman in a monogamous marriage (cf. Genesis 2:18; 1:28; Matthew 19:5–6). It forbids adultery (Exodus 20:14; Hebrews 13:4), sex before marriage (1 Corinthians 7:1–2), and all other forms of sexual immorality (1 Corinthians 6:18; 1 Thessalonians 4:3), including lust (Matthew 5:28).

As we have seen, each of these declarations and prohibitions is contradicted by the sexual immorality of our culture. If our society is right on sexuality, the Bible is wrong. If the Bible is wrong on sexuality, on what other subjects is it wrong? The satanic strategy of undermining God's word and truthfulness continues (cf. Genesis 3:1).

Second, it brands Christians as intolerant and oppressive, the topic of the next chapter.

Third, it threatens our religious freedom, a subject addressed in chapter 5.

Fourth, it convinces younger generations that our faith is irrelevant.

It should not surprise us that a society that rejects biblical morality is also rejecting biblical faith. The rise of the "nones" (those who say they have no religious commitment) is just one symptom of the narrative we have discussed. This narrative is clearly continuing. A play in honor of Pride Month depicted Jesus as transgender. A growing movement seeks to legalize prostitution. Advocates for polygamy and polyamory ("many loves") are gaining momentum. Next, we will see incestuous marriage. And we are already seeing the celebration of sexual relationships between people and animals (known as "zoophilia").

An observation often attributed to G. K. Chesterton notes, "When men choose not to believe in God, they do not thereafter believe in nothing, they then become capable of believing in anything."

In the guise of our greater metaphor, the issues we've so far discussed are tectonic plates that have pushed into one another over decades, revealing the fault lines of our culture. They created a domino effect: truth fell first; sexual liberation quickly followed. Then, as Christians have reacted to these issues, we've been branded as oppressive bigots.

Soon, we may be seen as dangerous adversaries to cultural progress who must be maligned or silenced.

"My schooling gave me no training in seeing myself as an oppressor."
— **PEGGY MCINTOSH**

3

The rise of Critical Theory: Are evangelicals oppressors?

In May 2021, the *Dallas Morning News* reported on a thousand-dollar gift given in support of Shannon Braun's campaign for her local school board. What made the story notable was the identity of the donor: Braun's brother, Chip Gaines, of *Fixer Upper* fame. What gave the story cultural notoriety was the later insinuation that the Gaineses, by supporting a family member, were also tacitly endorsing one aspect of that family member's platform: the prevention of teaching Critical Race Theory in that school district.

This story is one of many in the last few years in which Critical Race Theory (CRT) has played a sizable role. When last do you recall an academic theory having so much publicity and causing such divisiveness and rancor in the culture?

Our third earthquake is the rise of Critical Theory and how it can be used to characterize Christians as oppressors of all minority groups. To better understand this term, which is often politicized beyond its strict definition by all sides, let's review the history of "Critical Theory" (CT) and its evolution into Critical Race Theory.

What is Critical Theory?

"Criticism" has been described as "the application of principles or values in order to make judgments for the purpose of bringing about positive change." We are familiar with art critics, music critics, and so forth.

"Critical Theory" builds on this initiative in an extremely broad way. It is "a school of thought that stresses the examination and critique of society and culture, drawing from knowledge across the social sciences and philosophy." Its purpose is "explaining and transforming the circumstances that enslave human beings."

Until recently, CT was an academic theory discussed almost exclusively by academicians. However, its application to race in CRT has exploded into our cultural consciousness in recent years. The Black Lives Matter movement, the tragic death of George Floyd, growing concerns over policing of Black people, and the structural inequities that persist in our culture have all combined to make CRT a headline topic on a daily basis.

Schools, universities, and governmental agencies are teaching CRT or being prohibited from doing so. Corporations are holding seminars by CRT advocates. Churches and denominations are debating CRT and its biblical components or lack thereof.

Providing an in-depth analysis of CT and CRT is beyond the scope of this chapter. My purpose here is to offer a brief overview of CT and CRT, then connect their truth claims to the cultural antagonism rising against biblical Christians.

For purposes of brevity, I will confine my treatment of CT to Cameron Hilditch's overview in *National Review*, "How Critical Race Theory Works." Hilditch explains that Critical Theory was pioneered by a group of German Marxist thinkers known as the Frankfurt School. The group included Max Horkheimer, who first defined "critical" theory in a 1937 essay. He explained that it tries "to liberate human beings from the circumstances that enslave them" and "to create a world which satisfies" their "needs and powers."

According to Horkheimer, "critical" theory must provide an account with what is wrong with existing social arrangements, identify the agents of change, and provide achievable aims and standards against which these agents can measure their efforts.

In line with Marxist teaching, critical theorists view morality and human nature through the lens of social constructs. In their view, the shared interests of an oppressor class constrain and determine reality to a very high degree. Those who prosper have, by definition, organized the social order so as to exploit others and benefit themselves. Almost every social problem we face is therefore the fault of an oppressor class.

Critical theorists note that oppressors can be removed from power either through a democratic awakening among the masses or by revolutionary violence. Hilditch notes:

> The belief that reality is socially constructed is therefore a necessary premise of utopianism. It makes every bad outcome in society the fault of the people who constructed society in the first place. It imbues every tragedy or misfortune with malevolent agency and pernicious intent. It makes the problem of evil, which has plagued the downtrodden and perplexed the philosophers

since the dawn of time, ultimately the problem of
the existence of the oppressor.

If Critical Theory "makes the problem of evil . . . ultimately the
problem of the existence of the oppressor," who are the oppressors
according to Critical Race Theory?

What is Critical Race Theory?

For purposes of brevity, I will confine my treatment to Bruce
Ashford's excellent article in *Public Discourse* titled "Critical Race
Theory: Plundering the Egyptians or Worshiping Ba'al?" Ashford
notes that legal scholar Derrick Bell is usually considered the
founding father of CRT. In his 1970 book, *Race, Racism, and
American Law*, Bell argues that whites have always been racist and
allowed Black rights only when it benefitted whites to do so.

In his 1987 book, *And We Are Not Saved: The Elusive Quest for Racial
Justice*, he wrote even more explicitly: "Progress in American race
relations is largely a mirage obscuring the fact that whites continue,
consciously or unconsciously, to do all in their power to ensure their
dominion and maintain their control." Other scholars, especially
Kimberlé Crenshaw, Angela Harris, and Patricia Williams, built on
Bell's work by analyzing the "lived experience" of racial expression.

Richard Delgado and Jean Stefancic's reader *Critical Race Theory*
encapsulates the primary tenets of CRT. These authors argue that
racism is the everyday experience of Black Americans and other
non-white races. The idea of "race" is a social construction that
fostered a system of white ascendancy and continues to benefit
the dominant group. Because whites are the beneficiaries of this
prejudiced system, they are incompetent to speak about race or
racism. In addition, they are complicit in systemic racism to the
degree that they participate uncritically in the system.

Whites are therefore encouraged to participate critically in the public square by exposing the racial disparities that prevail in our nation's policing, sentencing, and incarceration. They are also encouraged to advocate for minorities' voting rights by eliminating gerrymandering and redlining (denying services to residents of certain areas based on their race or ethnicity) and by using legislation or social pressure to change speech norms that perpetuate racism.

CRT finds many supporters in the Black intellectual community, but many prominent Black thinkers reject it as a flawed theory, such as economists Thomas Sowell, Walter Williams, and Glenn Loury; political scientists Carol M. Swain and Wilfred Reilly; political commentators and activists Derryck Green and Alveda King; public intellectual Coleman Hughes; and elected official Tim Scott. They work to establish justice and promote activism but believe that CRT actually perpetuates racism and harms society.

In addition, many Christians acknowledge that CRT can be a useful tool for analyzing power dynamics but ultimately reject it as a worldview as fundamentally incompatible with the Christian faith. In their view, it functions as a form of intellectual idolatry and thus should be rejected.

Ashford lists four reasons why.

One: CRT identifies racism as the result of the West's historic cultural system rather than the corruption of an individual's heart.

According to CRT, each white citizen is implicated as a racist, whether or not he or she is personally prejudiced. The solution is to change the system and produce equity for all.

According to Scripture, sin is an individual's rebellion against God's word and will. Racism thus occurs when a person thinks, feels, acts, or speaks in a prejudiced manner toward another person merely because of that person's ethnicity. Racism is first and foremost a movement of the will.

CRT is helpful in exposing the degree to which individual sins can become incarnated in social structures and institutions. But CRT fails to note that individual repentance is essential to changing lives and social structures.

Two: CRT claims that "colorblindness" is impossible, so it promotes treating people differently on the basis of their ethnic heritage in order to privilege the oppressed and oppress the oppressor.

As Black sociologist George Yancey notes, this approach tends to ignore sins committed by minorities, which disempowers them by alleviating them of responsibility while alienating whites. By contrast, God's word applies to each of us based on our role and calling rather than our class or structural status.

Three: CRT functions as an ideology that locates salvation in society's liberation from injustice.

This is a form of anti-religion in competition with Christian orthodoxy. It has a "priesthood" of social and political influencers engaging in activism and leading revolutionary action. It seeks to use power to restrict certain racial groups while favoring others. It situates salvation within the physical world as society is liberated from its captivity to white cultural institutions.

By contrast, Scripture teaches that humans are finite and fallen, which means that we are incapable of creating pristinely just cultural institutions. We can reform existing institutions while striving for equality for all humans, no matter their ethnic heritage. But equity is not promised: even in heaven, some will possess more "crowns" than others and sit closer to Jesus' right hand than others (2 Timothy 4:7–8; Mark 10:40).

Four: CRT is a system of thought devoted to the idol of outcome equality. If someone fails to flourish, it holds that the primary reason for this must be that they are oppressed by an unjust system.

Ashford notes that CRT rightly recognizes oppression as evil and warns that individual sins and prejudices often coalesce in our society to warp and misdirect cultural institutions. As a result, we should work to bring healing and redirection to such embedded injustices.

However, because CRT conflicts with Scripture's overarching narrative, we should reject the temptation to accept it as a system of thought.

How do CT and CRT contribute to the tsunami?

We could say much more about CT and CRT in the context of biblical theology. For the present purposes, however, we'll confine our analysis to their participation in the antagonism rising against evangelicals today.

As we have seen, CT was developed in a Marxist worldview in which society consisted of classes in struggle with one another. Marxist scholar Cliff Slaughter states that, for Karl Marx, "class" is "rooted in social relations of production" and focuses on "conflict at the level of class (economic struggles which merge into the conflict between classes, which is organized through the political parties and the struggle for state power)."

Critical Theory proponents adapt this economic theory to social and political issues. In their worldview, a group with political or economic power is by definition the oppressor of those it used and oppressed. Christians have been the dominant religion in America since its founding and still hold significant positions of power across our culture (only two of our presidents made no formal affiliation with a specific Christian denomination). As a result, CT would cast Christians in the role of oppressors who must be oppressed by the oppressed.

In addition, CRT views racial minorities as specifically among the oppressed in American society. Since two-thirds of evangelical Christians are white, many CRT proponents view white evangelicals as oppressors who must be oppressed.

CT principles can clearly be applied to LGBTQ persons and issues as well. Since LGBTQ individuals comprise 5.6 percent of the American population, they are obviously a minority.

In addition, "intersectionality" theory describes such people as especially marginalized. According to law professor Kimberlé Crenshaw, who introduced the term, "intersectionality" is "a lens, a prism, for seeing the way in which various forms of inequality often operate together and exacerbate each other." She adds: "We tend to talk about race inequality as separate from inequality based on gender, class, sexuality, or immigrant status. What's often missing is how some people are subject to all of these, and the experience is not just the sum of its parts."

In this context, a person who is a racial minority or female and is also LGBTQ is especially marginalized. Since evangelicals who stand for biblical morality clearly stand against LGBTQ ideology, we are once again cast as the oppressors of the oppressed.

The lingering effects of CRT

An academic philosophy need not be understood in detail to become influential. For example, I have met few Americans who have read Immanuel Kant's *Critique of Pure Reason*. However, many are influenced by his assertion that we cannot know the "thing in itself" since "truth" for us is the subjective product of our minds interpreting our senses. Few have read Friedrich Nietzsche's *Thus Spoke Zarathustra*, but many agree that the desire for power motivates cultural "oppressors" today.

As CT and CRT become more widespread in education, corporate diversity training programs, and the larger culture, we can expect its tenets categorizing evangelical Christians as oppressors to become more pervasive and persuasive. It is tragically true that some Christians have used their position to oppress people in the past (the Crusades, the Inquisition, and support for slavery are obvious examples). However, CRT proponents claim that *all* Christians today are oppressors because we believe in the Bible, which has been used to oppress others.

This narrative will be especially powerful for younger adults and students. Combined with the claims that truth is subjective and sexuality is personal, the accusation that evangelicals are oppressors of persecuted minorities will further embolden our opponents in the coming years.

Chip and Joanna Gaines are but one example. As Christians who became famous due to their home-design show, they are highly visible targets for a culture that would prefer them to operate by its "rules" rather than by biblical standards.

When interviewed in June 2021 by *The Hollywood Reporter*, a teary-eyed Joanna Gaines said, "The accusations that get thrown at you, like you're a racist or you don't like people in the LGBTQ community, that's the stuff that really eats my lunch—because it's so far from who we really are. That's the stuff that keeps me up."

"I expect to die in bed, my successor will die in prison, and his successor will die a martyr in the public square. His successor will pick up the shards of a ruined society and slowly help rebuild civilization, as the church has done so often in human history."

—ROMAN CATHOLIC CARDINAL FRANCIS GEORGE OF CHICAGO IN 2010

4

The rise of secular religion: Are evangelicals dangerous?

The United Nations Committee on the Rights of the Child issued a stinging rebuke of the Catholic Church over its response to the clergy abuse scandal. That's not surprising news. Here's what is surprising: the UN commission also chastised the Church for its positions on abortion, contraception, and homosexuality. This was the first time the United Nations had pressured the Church to change its long-held beliefs, claiming that these beliefs are actually dangerous. They charged that the Church's positions on these issues harm people and must be altered.

As we have seen, there was a day when the church was recognized as the leading authority in Western culture. Then Christianity became marginalized, widely viewed as irrelevant but tolerated as harmless. Now the faith has become dangerous in the eyes of many, an aberration that must be opposed and even eradicated.

Richard Dawkins calls religion "the root of all evil" and describes it as a "virus" in the software of humanity that must be expunged. Christopher Hitchens's international bestseller, *god is not Great*, states in its subtitle that "religion poisons everything." Sam Harris claims that "science must destroy religion."

Albert Mohler notes: "The Christian church has long been understood by the culture at large to be the guardian of what is right and righteous. But now the situation is fundamentally reversed. The culture generally identifies Christians as on the *wrong* side of morality. Those who hold to biblical teachings concerning human sexuality are now deposed from the position of high moral ground" (his emphasis). He adds: "The moral revolution is now so complete that those who will not join it are understood to be deficient, intolerant, and harmful to society."

How did we come to this place? What does it mean for you and the future of our faith and culture?

How we got here

I'm old enough to remember when stores were closed on Sunday out of respect for God and because so many people went to church. Billy Graham was named one of the "most admired" men in America an unequaled fifty-seven times. A pastor was the "parson," the leading "person" in the community. Presidents, Supreme Court justices, senators, and congressmen were nearly always people of active Christian faith, at least in their public profile. The vast majority of Americans called themselves Christians.

Then, as we have noted, the church began losing its position of respect and relevance. Postmodernism convinced us that there is no such thing as absolute truth, making the Bible a diary of religious experience rather than the objective word of God. Relativism convinced us that there are no objective values, that you have no right to force your beliefs on me. Pluralism convinced us that there is no one right religion. As more and more Americans began encountering other world religions, they came to believe that Christianity is just one way to God, that the various religions are different roads up the same mountain. It doesn't matter what you believe, so long as you're sincere and tolerant—or so we've been told.

The sexual revolution of the 1960s called into question the church's moral authority. *Roe v. Wade* contradicted the Catholic Church's position on conception. Clergy moral failures continue to make headlines. It became conventional wisdom that the church is largely irrelevant to modern life.

But now we're seeing another shift: the Christian church is not just irrelevant—it's dangerous. Its beliefs must be opposed as actively and strongly as possible.

Part of this movement is the expression of personal animosity toward the Christian faith. For example, atheist Richard Dawkins is famous for his T-shirt, "Religion: Together we can find the cure." In *The God Delusion*, he calls the God of the Old Testament "a petty, unjust, unforgiving control-freak; a vindictive, bloodthirsty ethnic cleanser, a misogynistic, homophobic, racist, infanticidal, genocidal, filicidal, pestilential, megalomaniacal, sadomasochistic, capriciously malevolent bully." In his mind, and in the minds of many like him, faith in such a deity should no longer be tolerated by modern society. His call is being heard loud and clear in America.

For others, the attack on Christianity as dangerous is part of a secular movement that seeks to remove and replace our faith with its own ideology. Psychiatrist Robert Coles notes: "The secular mind in the past lived side by side with the spiritual interests and yearnings of millions, a sacred mind. In recent centuries that secular mind has itself experienced a transformation. Once an alternative to entrenched religious life, that secularity became an aspect of individualism, as societies became less and less dominated by church life, more and more capitalistic in nature."

Sociologist Philip Rieff described the era when the Christian movement began as the "first culture." It was dominated by a pantheon of gods whose followers were content with their religion and not missionary toward the larger world. According to Rieff, the Christian movement sparked a monotheistic and evangelistic "second culture" which swept away the "first culture."

Now we are in what Rieff calls the "third culture," which Australian pastor Stephen McAlpine describes as "hermetically sealed off from anything transcendent." It "recognizes only horizontal identity constructions, not vertical ones. Here is where meaning is determined, and here is where authority lies. It is ours to construct—and deconstruct." McAlpine adds: "This third culture is highly evangelistic and actively hostile to second-culture values."

For example, it considers sexual "freedom" and "authenticity" to be vital to personal and social flourishing. Biblical morality is therefore seen as dangerous to society and potentially deadly to LGBTQ individuals. The same vitriolic stance is taken with regard to abortion, euthanasia, or any other personal "freedoms" that are "threatened" by biblical faith. According to McAlpine, this is a "new religion" and rival gospel "the church has not encountered before."

This "new religion" seeks nothing less than to replace Christianity with its secular vision for a better future.

Discriminating against Christians

John Allen, a respected international journalist, calls the global persecution of Christians "the most dramatic religion story of the early twenty-first century, yet one that most people in the West have little idea is even happening." According to Allen, "Christians today indisputably are the most persecuted religious body on the planet."

In recent years, we have seen this pattern emerge in the US as well.

While he was still governor of New York, Andrew Cuomo spoke out against "extreme conservatives who are right-to-life, pro-assault-weapon, anti-gay," claiming that they "have no place in the state of New York." Note that he considers those who believe life begins at conception (a position consistent with his own Roman Catholic Church) to be "extreme" conservatives. New York City Mayor Bill de Blasio defended the governor's comments as "absolutely right." It is interesting that Cuomo believed he could dictate who has a "place" in his state. If an evangelical Christian were to make such a statement, what would be the reaction?

Former ESPN commentator Chris Broussard stated that Jason Collins, an NBA player who came out as gay, was living in "open rebellion to God." He was called a bigot and purveyor of hate speech. Family Research Council spokesman Peter Sprigg commented: "In the current culture, it takes more courage for someone like Chris Broussard to speak out than for someone like Jason Collins to come out." Illustrating his point, the Southern Poverty Law Center in Alabama branded Sprigg's organization as a hate group.

Many Christians in the academic world face ridicule for their faith. For instance, Elaine Howard Ecklund, a professor at Rice University, polled 1,700 scientists at elite universities. She discovered that, contrary to stereotype, nearly half say they are religious. But they practice a "closeted faith": "They just do not want to bring up that they are religious in an academic discussion. There's somewhat of almost a culture of suppression surrounding discussions of religion at these kinds of academic institutions." Each person she interviewed insisted on anonymity.

A US Army Reserve training presentation called evangelical Christians "religious extremists," listing them alongside al-Qaeda,

Hamas, and the Ku Klux Klan. A fourteen-year-old honors student and football player at Western Hills High School in Ft. Worth, Texas, was suspended for telling a friend in class that he was a Christian and believed that "being a homosexual is wrong." After legal counsel intervened, the suspension was reversed.

A nineteen-year-old student was told by a supervisor at California's Sonoma State University that she could not wear her cross while working at the school's freshman orientation. The university later apologized.

A report prepared by the Family Research Council and the Liberty Institute listed these examples of rising discrimination against Christians:

- A high school valedictorian in Victor, Iowa, was told he had to give a "secular" speech after he wanted to attribute his success to his faith in Christ.

- A Cisco employee was fired for expressing his views on traditional marriage in a book he wrote, even though he never voiced these opinions at work.

- An eight-year-old was barred from singing "Kum Ba Yah" at a Boys and Girls Club in Port Charlotte, Florida, because the song includes the words *Oh, Lord.*

- A nurse in Manhattan was forced to participate in a late-term abortion against her religious convictions lest she face the loss of her job and license.

A group calling itself "Angry Queers" claimed responsibility for throwing baseball-sized rocks through nine church windows in Portland's Mars Hill Church, including two one-hundred-year-old stained glass panes. They stated their hope that this "small act of vengeance will strike some fear into the hearts" of Christians who teach biblical morality. Rather than discuss their differences with the church, the group states, "The only dialog we need with scum like Mars Hill is hammers through their windows."

Christian Liberty Academy in Arlington Heights, Illinois, planned an event to discuss the homosexual activist agenda and honor a pro-family activist. After its glass entry door was smashed by bricks, the perpetrators warned, "If this event is not shut down, and the homophobic day trainings do not end, the Christian Liberty Academy will continue to be under constant attack."

The US Department of Justice and the Federal Bureau of Investigation reported 218 hate crimes against Christians in 2019. They included physical assault, theft and robbery, damage to property, arson, and threats and threatening behavior.

The *Wall Street Journal* headlined on July 22, 2020, "Desecration of Catholic Churches Across U.S. Leaves Congregations Shaken." Two days later, the *Tennessee Tribune* reported on recent crimes:

- A statue of Jesus was decapitated in Miami.

- An antiabortion memorial was damaged in New York.

- Virgin Mary statues in Colorado, Massachusetts, and Tennessee were desecrated.

- The doors of a Connecticut church were painted with "anarchist and satanic symbols," according to the Archdiocese of Hartford.

- A crucifix in Illinois was vandalized.

- St. John's Episcopal Church near the White House and St. Patrick's Cathedral in New York City were vandalized during protests following George Floyd's death.

Catholic League President Bill Donohue said of this violence, "It's all driven by hatred. Every last bit of it is driven by hatred."

Censoring Christians

The censorship of biblical morality is especially escalating in our day.

The Daily Citizen is a publication of Focus on the Family. On January 19, 2021, it tweeted that President Joe Biden's nominee for assistant secretary of health, Rachel Levine, is "a transgender woman, that is, a man who believes he is a woman." The story included a link to an article about the nomination. As a result, Twitter locked the magazine out of its account, informing the publication that its tweet violated Twitter's user rules forbidding "hateful conduct" and violence.

The magazine insisted that it never promoted violence: "As a Christian organization, we would never do so. We simply explained to our readers the appointment and defined what transgender women are—those born male who believe they are a woman, regardless of whether they have had opposite-sex hormones or surgeries. We believe Twitter's blocking of this tweet and lockdown of our account discriminates against Focus on the Family's The Daily Citizen on the basis of our religious affiliation." The platform rejected the appeal and said its ban would not be overturned.

In related news, a New Testament professor at Houston Baptist University was suspended from Facebook for voicing disagreement with President Biden's executive order allowing trans-identifying individuals to serve in the US military. Robert Gagnon (Ph.D., Princeton Theological Seminary) is a well-known scholar on the subject of human sexuality. He was locked out of his Facebook account for twenty-four hours after he posted a comment defending a friend who posted a satirical comment about the executive order.

In his post, Dr. Gagnon said the executive order will endanger women. He likened transgender ideology to a "religious cult" and said it "is indeed a pseudo-science" in that it forces people to reject basic biology. Facebook notified him that his words violated their "Community Standards on violence and incitement."

Dr. Gagnon responded, "There was absolutely no incitement to violence on our part. We abhor violence done to any person. This is just a thinly veiled and pathetic excuse for censorship of any critical views toward trans-tyranny over our consciences, religion, and reason." After his suspension was lifted, Dr. Gagnon posted on his page, "We are in the midst of rapidly accelerating public censorship of our views."

Renowned Princeton professor Robert P. George condemned Facebook's attack on Dr. Gagnon: "Censorship on Facebook and some other social media has now gone way beyond the bounds of the reasonable." He added, "People need to be able to criticize and forcefully challenge ideas—including ideas that are dominant in elite sectors of the culture and among people in the tech industry. What we do NOT need is the silencing of dissent." He warned, "Once it starts and becomes normalized . . . things do not end well."

Twitter's rules include this statement regarding "hateful conduct": "You may not promote violence against, threaten, or harass other people on the basis of race, ethnicity, national origin, caste, sexual orientation, gender, gender identity, religious affiliation, age, disability, or serious disease." The platform adds that it prohibits "content that intends to dehumanize, degrade, or reinforce negative or harmful stereotypes about a protected category."

Facebook similarly defines hate speech as "a direct attack against people—rather than concepts or institutions—on the basis of what we call protected characteristics: race, ethnicity, national origin, disability, religious affiliation, caste, sexual orientation, sex, gender identity, and serious disease." Such an "attack" includes "violent or dehumanizing speech, harmful stereotypes, statements of inferiority, expressions of contempt, [and] disgust or dismissal."

Let me be clear: no one should do what Twitter and Facebook prohibit. Christians should be especially adamant here, remembering that God's word explicitly forbids slander (Psalm 101:5; Proverbs 10:18) and commands us, "Do not speak evil against one another" (James 4:11).

Here's the problem: biblical morality with regard to LGBTQ behavior is considered "hateful conduct" by some LGBTQ persons. They view biblical prohibitions against homosexual activity as homophobic prejudice. If an individual claims that an article expressing such prohibitions is "dehumanizing speech" or a statement of "inferiority," that article could be blocked by social media. Even if the writer avoids any language that could be objectively viewed as hateful, the expression of biblical morality could be enough to provoke censorship.

Why religion is considered dangerous

The pattern of aggression against evangelicals is clear and escalating. Why? How has a faith that was respected and trusted become so vilified?

Religious beliefs are hazardous

"Angry atheists" such as Richard Dawkins were crusading against religion long before 9/11. However, this horrific tragedy gave them an unprecedented platform for their complaints. For others, the Holocaust furnishes grounds for disbelief.

Tragically, crimes in the name of religion are a tragic part of the human story. Cain killed Abel, apparently out of anger over a religious sacrifice that was not accepted (Genesis 4:1–8). Tribal warfare played a regrettable but significant role in the growth of early Islam. Wars between Hindus and Buddhists have marked their relations across their joint history. The Crusades were undoubtedly the most horrific chapter in Christian history.

Such a litany continues in our day with clergy abuse scandals making headlines, moral failures by respected Christian leaders, and allegations of racism and misogyny against denominational officials.

Religion is based on illusion

A second objection is the allegation that because religion makes claims that cannot be verified scientifically, it is based on illusion rather than evidential fact. We're told that statements, to be meaningful, must be capable of verification (the so-called "verification principle" in philosophy). Since religious statements cannot be verified beyond doubt by logic or experience, they are meaningless.

However, the verification principle cannot itself be verified. It is an axiom, an unverifiable presupposition. In that sense, it is like mathematical axioms. We cannot prove empirically that two parallel lines never intersect unless we are prepared to draw them forever. We cannot prove that $2 + 2 = 4$ rather than 5.

Are proponents of the verification principle prepared to call their assertion an illusion? Would they say the same of mathematics?

Religious beliefs are irrational

A third objection is that religion is dangerous because it is irrational, replacing facts and evidence with blind acceptance of theological assertions. Such critics often claim that the Enlightenment replaced "Dark Ages" mythology with "pure reason." They want our culture to affirm such reason and thus be "enlightened."

The Age of Enlightenment (from the seventeenth to nineteenth centuries) was actually, upon review, far less enlightened than these skeptics seem to admit. Keith Ward describes the era: "It was more obviously an age of increasingly aggressive nationalism ending in two world wars, repeated revolutionary conflicts, imperial expansion, the expansion of human slavery to industrial and global proportions, and violent political radicalism set against repressive absolutist monarchies."

He notes that, as the Enlightenment progressed, "Barbarism did not decrease. In the twentieth century it reached heights never previously imaginable. Where religion was restricted, as it was in National Socialist Germany, or even abolished, as it was in revolutionary France and Russia, what superseded it was cruel and inhuman to an unprecedented degree."

I have visited Cuba ten times and have seen firsthand the results of Castro's cultural revolution. His atheistic worldview and economic system have led to widespread famine, horrific financial deprivation, and minimal health care for the vast majority of Cubans. Those who are part of the Communist Party elite, by contrast, live in luxury.

Religious worldviews can be as reasonable as any other worldviews, as all are based on unprovable axioms. Christians cannot prove God exists, but atheists cannot prove that he does not.

Copernicus was a lay canon of the Catholic church; Kepler believed that the heavens reveal the glory of God; Newton believed that God created the laws of nature which scientists "discover." Francis Collins, head of the National Institutes of Health, is both a world-class scientist and a devout Christian.

Claiming that "religion is irrational" is an example of irrational thinking.

We have evolved beyond religion

A fourth argument against religion is the claim that it originated in the earliest stages of human development as a product of beliefs we now know to be superstitious or mythological. For instance, some skeptics claim that humans evolved from animism (worshiping the spirits in nature) to theism.

However, we have almost no evidence as to how our earliest ancestors interpreted their religious beliefs, as they have left us little more than archaeological remains. How did the inhabitants of Easter Island view their monoliths? This is question is still hotly debated.

In fact, the earliest written religious records we possess preserve religious worldviews very similar to ours today. Orthodox Jews still view the Torah as God's law for life; modern-day Hindus still use the same ascetic disciplines as those reflected in their ancient literature. And so-called "ancient" beliefs such as animism are still to be found in some parts of the world. I encountered such beliefs when serving as a missionary on the island of Borneo.

The claim that we have evolved beyond religion sounds plausible until we examine the evidence. Then we discover precisely what critics of religion claim for our beliefs: that they are based on supposition, not fact.

Belief in an afterlife is harmful in this life

We'll close with a fifth skeptical claim: that belief in an afterlife is harmful to this life and world. Supposedly those who believe in life after this life are less likely to maximize their experience in this world. They will use religion as an "opiate of the people" (Karl Marx), a tool for oppressing those who endure such suffering in expectation of heavenly reward. And they will sacrifice themselves and others in expectation of divine blessing (e.g., radical Muslim terrorists).

Actor George Clooney expresses well this conviction: "I don't believe in Heaven and Hell. I don't know if I believe in God. All I know is that as an individual, I won't allow this life—the only thing I know to exist—to be wasted."

Evangelicals are facing a secular ideology that functions as a religion aimed solely at earth. It intends to remove and replace any religion that endangers its vision for the future. For this reason, Christians are now "dangerous" to society.

As Richard Dawkins claimed, we must be "expunged."

If the culture at large believes that Christians are intolerant, irrelevant, oppressive, and dangerous, what happens next? How will these four convergent quakes affect our world and our witness?

And is the coming tsunami inevitable?

Has it already landed?

PART 2

Ideas have consequences

"A man may die, nations may rise and fall, but an idea lives on."

— JOHN F. KENNEDY

Next to my father's early death, the greatest pain of my life was watching our older son go through treatments for cancer. He had a small growth on the right side of his face near his jawline. His wife is the daughter of a physician and was in dental school at the time. She insisted that he get a sonogram, which was inconclusive. He then came to Dallas for a biopsy.

My wife and I were watching television on Friday night when he called us with the news that the growth was malignant. He had been diagnosed with acinic cell carcinoma, one of the rarest of all cancers. A surgeon removed as much as he could, but the tumor was Stage 2 and affected the nerves. Our son then underwent six weeks of radiation to remove the rest of the malignancy. To our unspeakable relief, the surgery and radiation were successful in removing the cancer. However, it can return, so he is tested annually.

His experience reinforced this fact: realities we do not see today can produce consequences that change our world tomorrow.

The four "earthquakes" we have identified and explored are more or less obvious to you depending on your vantage point.

- You may have little experience with "postmodern relativism," though you are likely familiar with the idea that truth is subjective.

- You are witnessing daily the consequences of the sexual revolution, though its beginnings and its future may be more opaque.

- You have likely heard of "Critical Theory," though its background and larger claims may be less apparent.

- The rise of secular "religion" is more obvious symptomatically than systematically.

But today's unnoticed realities can irrevocably alter our world tomorrow.

In Part 2, we will look at such consequences by asking four specific questions:

- Is religious freedom in jeopardy?

- Are evangelicals, churches, and schools at risk?

- Are evangelical leaders under attack?

- What is the risk to evangelicals in health care?

These consequences form the tsunami that I believe poses a threat to evangelicals and our larger culture. None arose in a vacuum. As surely as underwater shockwaves ripple water into immense waves, the ideas and events we have discussed have produced these consequences as symptoms of our larger cultural trajectory. But understanding these consequences is vital to responding to them in a redemptive way, the larger purpose for which this book is intended.

"As the union between spiritual freedom and political liberty seems nearly inseparable, it is our duty to defend both." —**THOMAS PAINE**

5

The Equality Act: Is religious freedom in jeopardy?

John Sherwood is the seventy-one-year-old minister of the Penn Free Methodist Church in north London. On April 23, 2021, he was preaching in public on God's design for families to have a mother and a father rather than two parents of the same gender. He cited the final verses of Genesis 1 as his text.

Police approached Rev. Sherwood and told him that three complaints had been received about his preaching. They accused him of causing "alarm and distress" to members of the public and urged him to come down from the stepladder on which he was preaching.

He politely declined, informing them that he had freedom of speech and that people have the freedom to ignore him if they wished. He resumed preaching, and onlookers again accused him of making homophobic statements and hate speech. The officers then pulled him down from the ladder and arrested him.

Is a day coming when biblical Christianity will be illegal in America?

When he wrote the majority opinion in the 2015 Supreme Court five-to-four decision legalizing same-sex marriage (*Obergefell v. Hodges*), Justice Anthony Kennedy assured Americans: "It must be emphasized that religions, and those who adhere to religious doctrines, may continue to advocate with utmost, sincere conviction that, by divine precepts, same-sex marriage should not be condoned. The First Amendment ensures that religious organizations and persons are given proper protection as they seek to teach the principles that are so fulfilling and so central to their lives and faiths, and to their own deep aspirations to continue the family structure they have long revered."

A nation that enshrined the freedom of religion in its Constitution would seemingly be the last place where such freedom would be in jeopardy. However, if the so-called Equality Act becomes law, this freedom will be lost for millions of evangelicals.

What is the "Equality Act"?

The Equality Act has been called "the most invasive threat to religious liberty ever proposed in America." In brief, it would amend the Civil Rights Act of 1964 by forbidding discrimination on the basis of sexual orientation and gender identity. In addition, this is crucial: the Act forbids appeal to the 1993 Religious Freedom and Restoration Act (RFRA) on the part of individuals or organizations.

Here's what this means in practice:

- Faith-based hospitals and insurers could be forced to provide gender-transition therapies that violate their religious beliefs.

- Children could seek to change their gender without parental knowledge or consent.

- Faith-based adoption and foster care agencies could be forced to place children with same-sex couples or lose their licenses.

- The Act would dismantle sex-specific facilities, sports, and other spaces. As a result, biological females would be forced to compete in sports with biological males and for athletic scholarships. Sexual assaults on girls in bathrooms and showers could escalate.

- Faith-based schools and businesses could be forced to violate their beliefs regarding homosexual activity and LGBTQ behavior or face fines, censure, or worse.

- Churches that rent their facilities to the public could be forced to rent them for same-sex marriages and other LGBTQ events.

David S. Dockery, the Distinguished Professor of Theology at Southwestern Baptist Theological Seminary and a longtime leading voice among evangelical scholars, writes: "The Equality Act would become the first major piece of legislation in the history of the United States to exclude protections for religious freedom. The bill does not even recognize the sacred rights of religious congregations, communities, or denominations. In fact, it would discriminate against people of faith by adversely affecting religious schools, benevolence organizations, women's sports, sex-specific facilities, and conscience rights."

The threat to Christian schools

The Alliance Defending Freedom (ADF) warns that the Equality Act "threatens religious colleges and universities, forbidding college students from using their federal tuition assistance at schools that 'discriminate' on the basis of sexual orientation or gender identity. That means any Christian university that has a code of conduct prohibiting sex outside of marriage or that declines to let biological males compete on women's sports teams could lose federal student aid."

Seven out of every ten students who come to a Christian college, including those who are racial minorities or come from poor families, receive some form of federal funding. The Act would interfere with their ability to choose the kind of educational context they believe serves them best and severely damage the capacity of these institutions to operate.

Christian schools, churches, and ministries would also be prohibited from discriminating against an employee on the basis of gender identity or sexual orientation with regard to hiring, firing, or promotion. Transgender individuals would be able to compete in athletic programs and access locker rooms and restroom facilities consistent with their gender identity.

The Equality Act would also jeopardize Christian colleges' ability to maintain their stated mission in presenting themselves to accreditation institutions. They would become pariah organizations within American higher education, jeopardizing their ability to serve the larger public good of society.

The threat to Christian employers and employees

Title VII of the 1964 Civil Rights Act prohibits employers from discrimination with regard to race, color, religion, sex, or national origin. In 2020, the US Supreme Court ruled (*Bostock v. Clayton County, Georgia*) that this prohibition extends to sexual orientation and gender identity. According to the Church Law Center of

California (CLCC), the Equality Act would codify *Bostock* by protecting LGBTQ employees from being fired or disciplined based on their sexual orientation or gender identity.

Dr. Dockery states: "The Equality Act expands the meaning of public accommodations in ways that would violate the privacy of women and men, forcing a gender ideology not only on schools, but healthcare organizations and those who provide benevolence and charitable services. Some entities that would not normally be classified by law as public institutions will be considered such by [the Act]. As a result of this legislation, if a Jewish synagogue, for example, rents its banquet hall for certain events, then they would be mandated to host events that they may consider immoral in their facility."

He adds this ominous warning: "This legislation would create a hostility toward religious ethics in the court of public opinion resulting in the narrowing of opportunities for people of faith to serve in the areas of education, social work, counseling, healthcare, as well as other spheres." He notes that "the missional, legal, financial, and cultural impact of the Equality Act on religious schools, non-profits, and benevolence organizations would be immediate and wide ranging."

And he adds that the Act "would change the way that graduates of religious colleges are viewed when it comes to graduate school opportunities, job placement, and internships, making it more difficult for these schools to carry out their mission in a faithful manner, limiting their ability to serve society at large. Frankly, the bill is so pervasive, almost nothing would escape its sweeping influence, having implications for private businesses and individuals as well."

The threat to Christians in health care

By adding "sex" to Title II of the 1964 Civil Rights Act on public accommodations, a "medical condition" such as abortion could be protected. As a result, a health care provider could be discriminating on the basis of sex if he or she refused to perform an abortion procedure. A hospital could be discriminating on the basis of sex if it refused to allow abortions within its facilities. And health insurance plans could be discriminating on the basis of sex if they did not include elective abortion coverage.

As an example showing the importance of appealing to the RFRA, a federal court ruled on January 19, 2021, that doctors could not be forced to perform transgender interventions that violate their sincerely held religious beliefs. The court cited the RFRA in issuing its ruling. If the Equality Act becomes law, such appeals would be prohibited. At this writing the Act has not passed the US Senate. If it does, President Biden has stated that he would sign it.

Explaining the opposition to biblical sexuality

President Biden is a practicing Catholic. Many who support the Equality Act are also practicing Christians. Given the large evangelical population in our country, coupled with the number of Catholics who support biblical sexual morality, why would Congress and the Biden Administration support legislation that assaults the religious freedoms of millions of Americans?

As we have seen, LGBTQ advocates see evangelical opposition as homophobic prejudice. They view us in the same way we view racial bigots. In their minds, our appeal to religious freedom is as repugnant as if we were members of the KKK citing religious freedom as a warrant for our horrific beliefs.

Extending this analogy, I'm sure you agree that racial discrimination is evil. Like you, I am convinced that racism should be repudiated and counteracted in every dimension of our society.

As a result, I would be deeply opposed if someone promoted racism by claiming biblical and religious warrant for their prejudice, demanded religious liberty protection for their beliefs, or built a massive media presence to promote their dangerous ideology. If they attempted "conversion therapy" aimed at changing the racial character of minorities, kept them from marrying people like themselves, or excluded them from adopting children, I would be similarly opposed.

Because I am convinced that racist ideologies and practices are dangerous to our nation and our future, I would support every legal response. For example, I would endorse school curriculum that taught racial inclusion and equality. I would limit racist exposure to the culture through social media and other platforms, ban racism in all governmental agencies and the military, and create pathways for racial minorities to marry and build families.

In short, I would characterize racists as social pariahs whose beliefs should no longer be tolerated by society.

Now, substitute LGBTQ equality for racial equality in the preceding four paragraphs. How we view racial bigotry is how many in our culture view our convictions regarding biblical sexual morality.

To this point, we are only seeing the first storm clouds of what I predict will become a hurricane of cultural rejection. For example, Facebook and Twitter have begun blocking posts critical of President Biden's transgender policy. National Religious Broadcasters, an evangelical association of Christian communicators, has begun tracking examples of social media and other online platforms restricting Christian viewpoints.

If the Equality Act passes the Senate in its current form and is signed by the president, we can expect such opposition to our beliefs and liberties to escalate legally as well as culturally.

Transgender rights and women's rights

One example of the impact of the Equality Act is the issue of transgender activism and women's rights. For my book 7 *Critical Issues*, I wrote a chapter-length examination of the transgender debate. For now, let's focus on one reaction to this issue.

Natasha Chart is executive director of the Women's Liberation Front, which she describes as a "radical feminist organization." She focuses on the government's order giving biological males who identify as women a pathway to compete in female sports and enter women's-only spaces such as bathrooms and showers. She raises concerns about the risk of injuries to females competing with biological males and girls being forced to shower with biological boys, among other issues. Then she warns:

> This is an emergency. We know parents are losing custody of their children for failing to affirm a gender identity. We know that minors are being sterilized. We know that girls and young women are losing out on athletic and college scholarship opportunities.
>
> We know that women in domestic violence shelters, in homeless shelters, in prisons are being terrorized by men who've been allowed to identify as women, and by officials who say, "Hey, it's out of our hands. He says he's a woman. He has to bunk with you."
>
> We think this is an emergency, and we would hope that everyone in politics would support women's side in this.

The Women's Liberation Front warns that the Equality Act would "end sports programs and scholarships set aside for women and girls. All such programs will have to admit men and boys who identify themselves as women or girls. Such programs will no longer meet their intended purpose of protecting the rights of women and girls by redressing historical inequality of opportunity." One writer adds that "a better name for this monstrosity of a law would be the 'Destroy Our Daughters Act.'"

The ADF reports that Pastor Esteban Carrasco and House of Destiny Ministries in Massachusetts wanted to open a women's shelter for survivors of domestic violence. However, state officials declared that churches are subject to state public accommodation laws. This means that churches that hold public activities— something as simple as a spaghetti supper—would be forced to open women's private changing areas and restrooms to biological men.

As a result, the House of Destiny Ministries would be forced to allow men who identify as women to use the same changing rooms, restrooms, and living facilities as the vulnerable women they sought to serve. Fortunately, in response to an ADF lawsuit, state officials reversed course, admitting that the First Amendment protects a church's freedom to operate consistently with its faith even when hosting community outreach events.

However, if the Equality Act becomes law, such freedom would be lost to churches and ministries.

I appreciate the American impulse to protect and support the rights of minorities, in this case the transgender population. And I want to state clearly that God loves all people, whatever their sexual orientation or gender identity (John 3:16). We are all broken people (Romans 3:23). We are all loved by the God who *is* love (1 John 4:8).

At the same time, transgender Americans constitute only 0.6 percent of our adult population. How do we also protect the rights of the majority?

"A perfect storm"

Os Guinness notes:

> The menace to religious freedom is no longer just the age-old evils of authoritarian oppression and sectarian violence around the world, but a grave new menace from within the West itself. For we are seeing an unwitting convergence between some very different Western trends that together form a perfect storm.
>
> One trend is the general disdain for religion that leads to a discounting of religious freedom, sharpened by a newly aggressive atheism and a heavy-handed separationism that both call for the exclusion of religion from public life. Another is the overzealous attempt of certain activists of the sexual revolution to treat freedom of religion and belief as an obstruction to their own rights that must be dismantled forever.

Guinness saw this "unwitting convergence" in 2013. What would he say of this "grave new menace" today?

Time will tell whether the Equality Act will become law in its present form and whether it will withstand legal challenges if it does. However, the larger trajectory it represents is clear and pervasive regardless of the outcome of this particular legislation.

A society built on freedom of speech and freedom of religion is now under siege from those who would sacrifice both to sexual freedom. As a result, the question of criminalizing Christian faith is no longer hyperbole.

An attorney speaking in a leadership consultation in which I participated explained our potential peril this way: Imagine that the Equality Act becomes law, but you refuse to amend your guiding documents to align with its requirements. A transgender individual wishes to participate in your activities according to their gender identity, but you refuse. They sue you and a judge issues an injunction. If you don't obey that injunction, someone goes to prison.

Neither the attorney nor I are claiming that such a future for biblical Christians is likely, but it is certainly possible. It reminds us once again that "all who desire to live a godly life in Christ Jesus will be persecuted" (2 Timothy 3:12).

Note the word *all*.

"The church is not a religious community of worshippers of Christ but is Christ himself who has taken form among people." —DIETRICH BONHOEFFER

6

Beyond the Equality Act: Are evangelicals, churches, and schools at risk?

A tsunami does not discriminate; it seeks to submerge anything blocking its path. By contrast, the spiritual tsunami threatening evangelicals is being guided and used by a very sophisticated and strategic Enemy.

The Bible warns us that "Satan disguises himself as an angel of light" (2 Corinthians 11:14). Jesus called him "a liar and the father of lies" (John 8:44). He is "the ruler of this world" (John 12:31); as such, "the god of this world has blinded the minds of unbelievers, to keep them from seeing the light of the gospel of the glory of Christ" (2 Corinthians 4:4).

Satan knows that attacking evangelicals can be a very effective way to deter us from our mission. He seeks to use those who reject biblical morality to lead this attack in the hope that our response will cause them to feel threatened in turn and drive them further from the gospel.

If religious freedom is at risk due to the Equality Act, how might similar policies affect us, our churches, and our schools? In addition to the Equality Act, evangelicals and evangelical organizations are under such attack in at least four ways.

The IRS and tax-exempt status

In June 2021, US Catholic bishops announced that they would prepare a document exploring whether priests can deny communion to politicians who support abortion. President Joe Biden and House Speaker Nancy Pelosi would be directly affected by this decision, as would other pro-abortion Catholics in public office. In response, Rep. Jared Huffman (D-Calif.) stated, "If they're going to politically weaponize religion by 'rebuking' Democrats who support women's reproductive choice, then a 'rebuke' of their tax-exempt status may be in order." Four days after the vote to prepare the document, the bishops released a statement saying "there will be no national policy on withholding Communion from politicians."

In related news, an organization called Christians Engaged applied for 501(c)(3) nonprofit status with the Internal Revenue Service. According to First Liberty, which is defending them, the organization "simply encourages citizens to pray for our nation and elected officials regularly, vote in every election to impact our culture, and engage in some form of political activity for the furtherance of the nation. It is nonpartisan and holds a weekly Bible study, sends weekly prayer alerts, and organizes statewide and area prayer gatherings to pray for local, state, and national government officials."

The IRS denied Christians Engaged's application. In its letter, it stated its reasons, among them: "You instruct individuals on issues that are prominent in political campaigns and instruct them in what the Bible says about the issue and how they should vote. These issues include the sanctity of life, the definition of marriage, and biblical justice. These issues generally distinguish candidates and are associated with political party platforms." The letter adds, "The bible [sic] teachings are typically affiliated with the Republican party and candidates. This disqualifies you from exemption under IRC [sic] Section 501(c)(3)."

These stories illustrate the possibility that churches and ministries that affirm biblical morality may not be able to obtain or retain nonprofit status in the future. I am not predicting this day since the political ramifications for the IRS and the federal government of threatening nonprofit status for the Roman Catholic Church and other Christian denominations are high. However, the cultural transformations we are discussing may make this strategy more plausible than ever before. And even if churches do not find their nonprofit status endangered, Christian ministries, schools, and other evangelical organizations could face such a threat.

Other legal threats

A legal challenge is being mounted at this writing against Christian colleges with regard to LGBTQ students. The Religious Exemption Accountability Project (REAP) filed a class-action lawsuit on March 26, 2021, alleging that the US Department of Education (DOE) was complicit "in the abuses that thousands of LGBTQ+ students endured at taxpayer-funded religious colleges and universities." REAP argues that under federal civil rights law Title IX, the DOE is obligated "to protect sexual and gender minority students at taxpayer-funded" schools, including "private and religious educational institutions."

The lawsuit's thirty-three plaintiffs include alumni and students from twenty-five colleges. Most are evangelical, including Liberty University and Baylor University, though the list includes one Mormon school and one Seventh-Day Adventist university. The implications of the lawsuit extend to more than two hundred religious schools that "discriminate" on the basis of sexual orientation. In 2018, these schools received $4.2 billion in federal aid.

In 1983, the Supreme Court ruled in *Bob Jones University v. United States* that Bob Jones University could not maintain its tax-exempt status while enforcing an interracial dating ban, even though the university claimed that the ban was based on its sincerely held religious beliefs. REAP cites this decision as precedent for its lawsuit. As with the Equality Act, the REAP lawsuit threatens Christian colleges and universities with the loss of federal scholarship funding and other similar effects.

One additional factor: the Education Department stated on June 16, 2021, that transgender students were protected under Title IX, the law that prohibits sex-based discrimination in federally funded schools. Education Secretary Miguel A. Cardona was asked how this announcement relates to bills being introduced around the country to bar transgender girls from playing sports. He replied, "The reality is each case has to be investigated individually." He asserted again that his department would not tolerate discrimination in schools receiving federal funds. At this writing, it is not known how this announcement will relate to evangelical colleges and universities.

Social and cultural threats

In addition to the Equality Act and other legislation, biblical Christian churches, schools, and individuals face an increasing variety of challenges from our anti-Christian culture and society.

For example, during the 2021 NCAA men's basketball tournament, a *USA Today* columnist complained that the NCAA allowed Oral Roberts University to compete. She accused the evangelical school of "deeply bigoted anti-LGBTQ+ policies" that "can't and shouldn't be ignored." In her view, the school's policies are "wildly out of line with modern society and the basic values of human decency." She argued that the NCAA should not have permitted the school's team to take part in the tournament.

Another *USA Today* article headlined "Don't use Dallas Cowboys' name, AT&T Stadium to mainstream anti-trans hate." The writer was protesting the fact that Promise Keepers, an evangelical ministry "focused on helping men live with integrity," announced an event in the stadium in July 2021.

Theological compromise

Another threat to churches, ministries, and schools comes from within. In response to the cultural narrative we've discussed, a growing number of leaders within these institutions are adopting positions that contradict the orthodox tenets of biblical morality as they have been understood and embraced for millennia.

- Catholic priests in Germany are defying a Vatican ban by blessing gay unions.

- A Baptist church in Indiana ordained a transgender pastor.

- A Methodist church in Illinois confirmed for ordination a gay man who is also a drag queen. He wore wigs and full makeup while participating in his church's "Drag Sunday" in April 2021.

The sexual revolution has influenced heterosexuals just as it has LGBTQ persons. *Christianity Today* reports that:

- 58 percent of white evangelicals and 70 percent of black Protestants believe cohabiting is acceptable if the couple plans to marry.

- 43 percent of evangelical Protestants ages fifteen to twenty-two said they definitely or probably would cohabit in the future; only 24 percent said they definitely would not.

- Over two-thirds of those ages twenty to forty-nine had cohabited at least once.

- And 53 percent of evangelical Protestants currently in their first marriage cohabited with each other before being married.

According to Pew Research Center, half of US Christians said casual sex between consenting adults is sometimes or always acceptable; 36 percent of evangelical Protestants agreed.

There are three ways Christian theologians and ministers can relate the Bible to the sexual revolution.

One response is to claim that the Bible is wrong.

I once heard a bishop in a mainline denomination claim categorically, "We now know that Paul was a homophobe." Theologian Walter Wink states, "The Bible clearly considers homosexuality a sin, and whether it is stated three times or three thousand is beside the point. . . . I freely grant all that. The issue is precisely whether that biblical judgment is correct." He proceeds to claim that it is not.

A second response is that we are wrong.

As we will discuss in chapter 10, Matthew Vines and David Gushee are examples of professing evangelicals who believe that the Bible does not forbid loving, monogamous homosexual relationships. They claim that the biblical era knew nothing of same-sex orientation, adding that the Bible prohibits sexual oppression and exploitation, not homosexuals living in a monogamous, covenant relationship.

A third response is that the culture is wrong.

As I will show in Part 3, the cultural onslaught against truth and biblical morality is tragically flawed and dangerous to our collective future.

Søren Kierkegaard observed, "Verily there is that which is more contrary to Christianity, and to the very nature of Christianity, than any heresy and schism, more contrary than all heresies and all schisms combined, and that is to play Christianity."

Rising opposition

It has been said that politics are downstream from culture. The political and legal challenges evangelicals are facing are themselves symptoms of cultural opposition to biblical truth and morality. And this tsunami stems from the four earthquakes we have discussed.

Left unchecked, the tide will continue to rise.

"A business, successful or not, is merely a reflection of the character of its leadership." —**TRUETT CATHY**

7

"Woke" business: Are evangelical leaders under attack?

More than four hundred companies have signed on to support the Equality Act. Their number includes Tesla, Pfizer, Delta Airlines, Starbucks, Home Depot, and Amazon. Burger King tweeted early in Pride Month that it would make a donation to the Human Rights Campaign for every chicken sandwich it sold.

When Georgia lawmakers enacted new voting regulations, Coca-Cola chairman and CEO James Quincey called them "unacceptable" and a "step backwards." In response, officials in Surry County, North Carolina, voted to remove Coca-Cola machines from all government facilities.

In celebration of Pride Month, The LEGO Group announced that it would produce a LEGO set in a variety of colors and physical characteristics to celebrate LGBTQ individuals. The creator of the series added that the purple figure is meant as "a clear nod to all the fabulous drag queens out there."

The pattern is clear: business is in the business of promoting social activism as never before. Why? How does this narrative impact Christian morality?

"The invisible hand of the market"

The Scottish Enlightenment thinker Adam Smith developed ideas that became foundational for what we know as the free market economy. His 1776 book, *An Inquiry into the Nature and Causes of the Wealth of Nations* (usually referred to simply as *Wealth of Nations*), is considered one of the most significant books in Western history.

In it and other writings, Smith introduced the concept of the "invisible hand," a metaphor for unseen forces that move the market. They include individual self-interest, freedom of production and consumption, and the best interests of society. Their interplay, along with other pressures on market supply and demand, produces the natural movement of prices and the flow of trade.

As a result of his work and that of other similar thinkers, the business climate in the United States developed with a general belief that voluntary private markets are more productive than government-run economies.

In such an economy, business leaders have an enormous influence on society. Since they own their private businesses, they can decide how to use them to engage with cultural issues. For the most part, successful business leaders have chosen to focus on business success. As the late economist Milton Friedman famously said, "The business of business is business." The financial bottom line was the measure of success. Creating value for shareholders and customers was paramount.

As a result, for most of my lifetime I could not have told you the personal or political beliefs of the nation's leading CEOs. In fact, I could not have named most of the nation's leading CEOs. Most business leaders focused on the profitability of their business and viewed personal visibility as detrimental to their corporate mission.

The bottom line is still the bottom line, but for reasons we discussed in Part 1, achieving it looks significantly different than it did just a few years ago.

What changed?

At least five forces have led to the rise of "woke" business in our day.

One: Younger employees have been educated in secular ideology.

As we have noted, it is conventional wisdom in our culture that truth is personal and subjective. Each person's truth is their truth. The exception is Critical Race Theory, which is convincing a generation that our nation was founded on systemic injustice that must be opposed on every level.

Younger employees steeped in this worldview understandably wish to confront such injustice in every dimension of their lives, including their vocations. They want their employers and the work they do for them to align with this mission. They often decide where to seek employment on this basis.

In fact, one report ranks workplace culture behind only work-life balance and pay as the highest priorities for young workers. In another survey, 76 percent of employees and job seekers said a diverse workforce was important when evaluating companies and job offers. Workshops are encouraging prospective employees to bring their "authentic self" to work.

Two: Employees view their employer
as a platform for their personal mission.

In *A Time to Build*, author Yuval Levin diagnoses the conflicts, rancor, and despair of our present culture as a failure of leadership. He notes that our institutions have historically served to mold the character of their members in line with their mission and values. From government and military to media, education, business, religion, and civic groups, these institutions had a clearly defined culture that shaped their employees and was served by their leaders.

I can testify personally to this fact. My father-in-law spent his entire career with IBM, rising to a place of significant leadership. He talked often about how IBM "did things," from the dress code (white dress shirts and ties) to employee relations and customer service. One who worked for IBM was expected to work the way IBM worked.

As Levin notes, this relationship between employer and employee has shifted dramatically in recent years. Many leaders now see their institutions as platforms for personal advancement and status. Their personal "brands" have become public and popular, tying them to the companies they lead, such as Apple CEO Tim Cook and the co-founder of Microsoft, Bill Gates.

Employees likewise see their employment as a platform for personal advancement and branding. Social media amplifies this relationship, giving everyone a platform for their personal opinions. As a result, companies whose leaders and employees are committed to "woke" ideology are being used to advance this ideology as never before. Corporate stands on issues ranging from election integrity to LGBTQ rights are common, as is product development that advances these agendas.

Three: Cancel culture is a very real threat.

Neil L. Golightly was communications chief for Boeing, where he was known for promoting female talent within the team and serving as an exemplary employee. Nonetheless, he resigned in 2020 after only six months on the job. The reason: an employee complained about an article he wrote in 1987 when serving as a pilot in the US Navy.

In the article, Golightly claimed that "introducing women into combat would destroy the exclusively male intangibles of war fighting and the feminine images of what men fight for—peace, home, family." When the article came to light last year, he stated that he disowned its arguments soon after writing it. He added that it is "painful because it is wrong. Painful because it is offensive to women. Painful because it reminds me of the sharp and embarrassing education the uninformed and unformed 'me' of that time received as soon as the piece appeared."

He also stated that people should have room to mature and change their ideas without being judged on opinions they held decades ago. Nonetheless, in accepting Golightly's resignation, Boeing's CEO stated, "I want to emphasize our company's unrelenting commitment to diversity and inclusion in all its dimensions."

"Cancel culture" has been described as "removing of support for public figures in response to their objectionable behavior or opinions. This can include boycotts or refusal to promote their work."

For example, Goya Foods CEO Bob Unanue appeared at a press conference with President Donald Trump in July 2020 and expressed gratitude for his leadership. Mr. Unanue was honored by President Obama in 2011 for his work with his administration. And Goya Foods donated two million pounds of food to food banks during the coronavirus pandemic. Nonetheless, when Mr. Unanue appeared with President Trump, there were immediate calls to boycott his company.

Company leaders understandably do not want to face boycotts and social media protests. As a result, they face increasing pressure to align their companies with agendas that ensure their acceptance by "woke" constituents.

Four: "Woke" business practices appeal to new customers.

Only 5.6 percent of Americans identify as LGBTQ, but nearly 70 percent support nondiscrimination protections for LGBTQ persons. This represents a very sizeable customer demographic.

As a result, "woke" practices that appeal to them are good for the bottom line. In contrast to the threat of cancel culture, this is a positive enticement for public alignment with LGBTQ ideology. We should therefore not be surprised by the plethora of toys, garments, and other merchandise displaying rainbow icons during Pride Month or the public statements by corporate CEOs on "woke" issues.

Just as businesses market to other demographics, they will market to those who support "woke" issues.

Five: Some business leaders genuinely embrace "woke" ideology.

Tim Cook has been CEO of Apple since 2011. Upon taking over the company from founder Steve Jobs prior to Jobs's death, he has advocated publicly for LGBTQ support. In 2014, he became the first chief executive of a Fortune 500 company to publicly come out as gay.

The next year, he wrote an op-ed for the *Washington Post* warning that "pro-discrimination 'religious freedom' laws are dangerous." In the article he stated, "On behalf of Apple, I'm standing up to oppose this new wave of legislation—wherever it emerges. I'm writing in the hopes that many more will join this movement." Above the article, the *Post* displayed in italics the words, "Tim Cook is chief executive of Apple."

Mr. Cook clearly believes personally in the LGBTQ ideology for which he advocates publicly. As Critical Theory is taught in more and more schools and the secular worldviews we've discussed in this book continue to proliferate, we should expect more CEOs to adopt their agendas professionally and publicly.

"Woke" business and social media

Social media platforms deserve special consideration in this regard since they are so dominant in our culture and so illustrative of our theme. Facebook, Twitter, Google, and other digital companies are privately owned. As a result, they have every legal right to decide what content they will allow on their platforms. If their leaders and editors consider biblical morality to be dangerous to society, they will predictably censor such content from their sites.

At Denison Forum, we would never allow a KKK member to publish an article on our website promoting white supremacy. This is how many of the social media platforms of our day view the biblical truths our ministry embraces. In addition, these platforms are widely considered to utilize algorithms that amplify "woke" voices while hiding or suspending content with which they disagree. The issue is so serious that it has led to several congressional hearings.

Why is "woke" business a threat for evangelicals?

It has always been true that private businesses can do whatever they wish with their businesses so long as they do not violate the law. However, we are now living in a culture where "woke" companies can do much to harm others within the law.

First, such business tactics are clearly intended to indoctrinate their customers.

Cereal boxes and children's cartoons celebrating LGBTQ ideology are aimed at the youngest and most vulnerable members of society. Using well-known companies to popularize "woke" social agendas similarly provides social proof intended to persuade consumers and the general public.

Since consumer spending comprises 70 percent of the US economy and the US is the largest advertising market in the world ($242.54 billion was spent on advertising to consumers in 2020), we should not be surprised that corporate businesses wield enormous cultural influence.

Second, businesses will become more doctrinaire as they increasingly employ those who advocate for "woke" ideologies.

As we have seen, many younger employees seek employers who advocate for social agendas which the employees support. They also view their employers as platforms for the personal expression of these agendas. We should expect this trend to continue and escalate.

Third, "woke" businesses can threaten employees and disenfranchise shareholders who disagree with their ideologies.

- Brendan Eich was CEO of Mozilla, a company known for its web browser. He was forced to resign when it was discovered that he had donated $1,000 five years earlier to a campaign seeking to ban same-sex marriage in California.

- A Christian in New Jersey filed a wrongful termination suit against Starbucks in November 2020, claiming that she was fired for refusing to wear the company's Pride shirt.

- A Christian physician assistant was fired in 2020 for refusing to provide off-label hormone therapy and invasive medical procedures for transgender patients, even though other medical professionals on staff were available to provide these treatments.

Jerry Bowyer describes himself as "chief economist for a financial firm that has substantial investments in a broad range of companies." He is also opposed to the so-called Equality Act on the grounds that it "directly and explicitly overrules the Religious Freedom Restoration Act" and believes that "companies should focus on business and not politics."

As a result, he attended several annual shareholder meetings to ask management about the Act. He writes, "In every case so far, the question I asked has not been answered on the call. That was disappointing enough in its own right, but in several cases, the companies in question did something particularly egregious: They implied or outright said that there were no more questions to answer, even though my question was never even acknowledged."

Fourth, "woke" businesses use money raised from evangelicals to advance agendas we may not support.

Pew Research Center estimates that evangelical Protestants comprise 25.4 percent of the American population. Pew also calculates that 42 percent of evangelical Protestants earn more than $50,000 a year. When we shop at stores that promote "woke" ideologies, our dollars go to promote these ideologies. When we use social media platforms that discriminate against biblical morality, our use of these platforms enables such discrimination.

"The great difficulty of our Christian calling"

With these words, the Rev. John Caird began a sermon on October 14, 1855, before Her Majesty the Queen and Prince Albert:

> To combine business with religion, to keep
> up a spirit of serious piety amidst the stir and
> distraction of a busy and active life—this is
> one of the most difficult parts of a Christian's
> trial in this world. It is comparatively easy to be
> religious in the church—to collect our thoughts
> and compose our feelings and enter, with an
> appearance of propriety and decorum, into the
> offices of religious worship, amidst the quietude
> of the Sabbath, and within the still and sacred
> precincts of the house of prayer. But to be religious
> in the world—to be pious and holy and earnest-
> minded in the counting room, the manufactory,
> the marketplace, the field, the farm—to carry out
> our good and solemn thoughts and feelings into
> the throng and thoroughfare of daily life—this is
> the great difficulty of our Christian calling.

How much more challenging is it to "combine business with
religion" today?

"Woke" business is both a symptom and a cause of secular aggression
against biblical truth and morality in our day. It is a symptom of
ideologies that consider personal authenticity and sexual "freedom"
to be the pathway to flourishing and that brand biblical morality
as dangerous to society. And it is a cause of such aggression as it
sponsors and popularizes this secular ideology.

Yet we are called as Christians "to be religious in the world" no
matter the turning tide of culture.

"We should be concerned not only about the health of individual patients, but also the health of our entire society." —**NEUROSURGEON BEN CARSON**

8

Designer babies and chimeras: What is the risk to evangelicals in health care?

Alexis Drutchas is a board-certified physician in family medicine and palliative care (medical care for those living with serious illness). In an op-ed for CNN, she asks, "Do adults with capacity hold the ultimate authority over their own bodies and the medical decisions for their minor children, or don't they?"

She is concerned about laws preventing what she calls "reproductive rights," "transgender health," and "aid in dying." As is typically the case, she uses euphemisms meant to convey the most positive sentiment to readers, but the "reproductive rights" she supports include abortion on demand; "transgender health" includes sex-change surgeries and similar procedures; and "aid in dying" is euthanasia.

She complains that those supporting such laws are "suggesting that there are 'right and wrong' choices rather than acknowledging that individuals have unique needs and the autonomy to make decisions that are right for them." She adds that "the continued promotion of paternalistic ideologies can frequently be traced back to religious fundamentalism."

In her view, "the central question" regarding these issues "is not only about human rights but also about empathy." I agree completely. However, the empathy I believe we should extend to patients looks very different from the empathy she champions.

If truth is subjective, as we discussed in chapter 1, ethics are subjective as well. If sexual "freedom" means doing anything you wish with your body and those who consent, biblical morality is irrelevant at best. If Christians are oppressors, then women who seek abortions, people seeking "gender-affirming" procedures, and patients seeking euthanasia are the oppressed. If a secular religion celebrating personal authenticity is replacing the Christian worldview, medical decisions will follow suit.

I have worked for years as an advisor on medical ethics with Christian hospitals and medical professionals. In this capacity, I see every day the rising challenges evangelicals face. What we are facing is true of all Christians in healthcare and Christians seeking health care as well. In fact, I believe that the culture wars we have been describing are nowhere clearer or more dangerous than in this context.

Consequences of the Equality Act

As we noted in chapter 5, the Equality Act would force faith-based hospitals and insurers to provide "gender-affirmation therapies" (sex-change procedures) that violate their religious beliefs. But this is only one consequence of the Act for evangelicals in healthcare.

The Act forbids discrimination based on "sex," including "pregnancy, childbirth, or a related medical condition." It states that "pregnancy, childbirth, or a related medical condition shall not receive less favorable treatment than other physical conditions."

In the past, when "sex" was added to federal law, Congress exempted abortion. The Act, when it refers to "a related medical condition," now includes abortion. By prohibiting reference to the Religious Freedom Restoration Act, the bill removes any religious or conscience protection for Christians.

Liberty Counsel Founder and Chairman Mat Staver writes, "This outrageous so-called 'Equality Act' will make abortion a federal right from conception to birth and will override every state law. It will force health care providers, pharmacists, hospitals, and crisis pregnancy centers to provide, participate in, or make abortion referrals. The bill will require state and federal funding of abortion and force employers and insurance carriers to cover abortion."

The Act, by elevating LGBTQ persons to protected-class status, would also require evangelical hospitals and care providers to offer reproductive services that violate their religious beliefs. Uterine transplants, in-vitro fertilization, and surrogacy resources are examples of services that would be required for lesbians and same-sex couples.

That said, our culture's insistence on personal autonomy and "authenticity" extends beyond pregnancy and gender-related issues. The following sections offer dozens of examples and hypotheticals because the speed of our scientific progress is outpacing the central ethical questions we should be asking—and answering—with regard to the broad-reaching implications of our technological advances. These issues are truly unseen seismic tremors that will significantly alter our cultural landscape in due time.

Genetic medicine

Francis S. Collins is head of the National Institutes of Health and formerly led the Human Genome Project. In his insightful book *The Language of Life: DNA and the Revolution in Personalized Medicine*, he writes: "Without question, man's knowledge of man is undergoing the greatest revolution since Leonardo." Dr. Collins is describing the advent of "precision" or "personalized" medicine, i.e., the use of genetics to prevent, diagnose, and treat disease. Let's consider some examples, discussing their enormous potential but also their grave consequences apart from clear and objective ethical guidance.

Prior to conception

Genetic screening prior to conception can tell prospective parents if they are carriers of mutant genes. For instance, the Jewish population is especially at risk for Tay-Sachs, an inherited disease that usually results in death by the age of four. In response, a community of Orthodox Jews in New York City developed a program called *Dor Yeshorim* ("the generation of the righteous") to discourage the marriage of young people found to be carriers of this genetic disorder. The program has greatly reduced the incidence of Tay-Sachs within the community and has been extended to screen for cystic fibrosis and Gaucher disease as well.

You can see the enormous potential of this technology for eliminating genetically inherited diseases. But consider some other implications:

- Imagine potential mates being chosen for their genetic capacities and reproductive potential. Will genetic information be analyzed before couples marry or even date?

- Is this the future of human progress, a kind of eugenics? Will pressure be brought increasingly to bear on couples to produce children in this way? Will parents face lawsuits from children whose diseases could have been corrected by such techniques?

- What are the implications for health care providers? Will physicians and hospitals be pressured to provide such services? Will they face litigation if they do not, or if their test results prove to be incorrect? How will they balance medical paternalism, doing what they know to be best for the patient, with the freedom of parents to bear children as they choose?

- Will this technique be used as a kind of evolution in which only the healthiest and most intelligent genes are transmitted? Will reproduction one day be taken from the bedroom and confined to the laboratory?

This is not the stuff of science fiction movies any longer but a very real possibility in the coming years.

For conception

As difficult as the ethics of precision medicine may be before conception, they become far more complicated when applied to conception itself.

Let's begin with assisted reproduction. One out of every one thousand pregnancies in America involves a disease that could have been predicted by carrier screening. "Assisted reproduction" is the umbrella term for a variety of medical techniques intended to produce a successful pregnancy:

- Artificial insemination: the use of donor sperm to inseminate the woman.

- *In vitro* fertilization: sperm and ovum are combined in the laboratory and then implanted in a woman's uterus.

- Pre-implantation genetic diagnosis (PGD): fertilized embryos are tested genetically for defects before being implanted.

Each of these techniques can be enhanced medically by genetic testing. One day it will be possible for donor sperm or eggs to be selected for their genetic traits. Athletes and scholars have been selling their sperm or eggs to banks for years; genetic screening will make them even more in demand.

It is estimated that one million embryos created by IVF that are yet to be implanted are currently in suspended animation around the country. If you believe that life begins at conception, as I do, then you must conclude that each of these lives was created and then frozen.

How will these developments affect the stem cell debate? Stem cells are unspecialized cells that can be promoted to become any of the 210 different kinds of tissues in the human body. Embryonic stem cells are especially pluripotent, capable of becoming anything needed. But to obtain them, we must kill an embryo.

How is genetic medicine relevant to this debate? On the positive side, stem cells could greatly enhance regenerative medicine. We can transplant stem cells today into patients suffering from conditions such as Parkinson's disease, diabetes, or a spinal cord injury. What if we could genetically engineer cells to fight an entire spectrum of diseases?

Will embryonic research labs produce millions of embryos for such use? Will we see embryos cloned to produce stem cells for transplant or for research to study a specific disease? Where is the line between sexual and asexual reproduction?

Abortion involves the destruction of a fetus; cloned embryos for research purposes would require such deaths. At what point would such reproduction be halted? Fourteen days? After organs have developed and can be used for transplantation?

How do these advances relate to organ donation? More than one hundred thousand Americans are currently on waiting lists for a donated organ. Will laboratories create embryos designed to produce stem cells as needed for specific issues? Will the parents of a child with leukemia be able to order stem cells engineered to that child's needs? Will parents be able to conceive children through IVF that will produce organs genetically engineered for transplant?

Will we see a day when a couple, or a mother, could sell such organs on the open market? The National Organ Transplant Act of 1984 prohibits the sale of organs for transplant. How will this law be enforced?

Consent has been necessary for organ donation in the past, either of the subject or of the immediate family. What of embryos, especially those conceived for purposes of research or organ creation?

The 1997 movie *Gattaca* envisions a world in which life begins in two ways: *in utero*, through natural means, and *in vitro*, through genetic engineering. Those who are engineered become superior members of society; those who are not are called "in-valids" and perform custodial work and other duties. Is this our future?

After conception

Today, you can send a swab of your saliva to services that will test it for genetic factors, traits, and possible disease markers. In the future, we will be able to diagnose thousands of diseases based on their genetic markers. And we will be able to do so immediately after conception, *in utero*.

Doctors will be able to tell parents if their unborn child has a tendency for obesity or diabetes so they can regulate diet and exercise. And we can start regimens *in utero* or immediately after birth as needed.

Currently, the blood of newborn babies is tested for a variety of inheritable diseases. Among these is PKU, an enzyme disorder that leads to severe retardation. If a PKU infant is placed immediately on a diet very low in phenylalanine, such an outcome can be prevented.

However, such capacities bring enormous ethical challenges. Will advances in neonatal genetic testing motivate even more abortions? For instance, testing for fragile X syndrome, the second most common cause of mental retardation, could lead to even more elective terminations of pregnancy.

If a fetus is found to have physical problems that can be affected by the mother's health, will she be required to behave in ways that will not prove harmful to the child? Will the child be able to sue her later if she does not? Will health care providers face litigation if they do not offer such diagnostic and treatment services or if they do not produce the desired results? When parents can discover nearly everything about their unborn child, will abortion rates skyrocket?

And consider the life of the individual versus the good of the whole. If genetic testing reveals that a baby would place a great strain on the economic and health care systems of the community, will there be increased pressure on the parents to abort?

After birth

Genetic medicine offers at least three very exciting possibilities for the treatment of disease after birth.

The first relates to medication. Adverse reaction to medication is one of the leading causes of death in America. With advances made by genetic medicine, medical scientists can eventually eliminate this issue as they target the specific genetic nature of the disease and prescribe medicines appropriate to it. And doctors will be able to help patients continue with their regimen. After two years, patients with a genetic diagnosis have shown more than 86 percent adherence to their treatment regimen compared to 38 percent prior to testing.

Second, conventional treatments will be enhanced greatly. For example, there are five types of colon cancer and at least ten different categories of breast cancer; what works for one does not necessarily work for another. Being able to focus treatments on the specific cancer based on its genomic sequence will enormously enhance patient experiences and outcomes.

Third, genetic treatments are in the future. Doctors may be able to substitute healthy genes for disease-causing genes, treating the cancer or other disease in new and much more effective ways.

However, ethical dilemmas exist here as well. When genetic testing reveals diseases that will begin later in life, how are we to respond? For example, Gaucher disease type I is typically diagnosed at age twenty-eight. How are doctors to handle such information when it becomes known at birth? If I knew that I would develop ALS in three years, leading to a terrible death and horrible burdens for my family, how might I respond? Will we see suicides and assisted suicides escalate?

Will medical advances make euthanasia easier to experience and practice? Will there be pressure brought to bear by families or society?

Other ethical issues

When it comes to personal ethics versus communal law, to what degree are these issues the subject of the state? Many in the pro-choice camp oppose abortion personally but do not want the state making such decisions for the mother. Will this thinking prevail with genetic medicine? Where and how?

Regarding privacy issues, who owns your tissue? Who should have access to your genotype results? How should that information be used? How does this issue relate to insurance, employability, and reproductive decisions?

Will genetic testing lead to discrimination by employers and insurers? In May 2008, President George W. Bush signed a bill making it illegal for employers and insurers to discriminate on the basis of genetic information. The Genetic Information Nondiscrimination Act encourages the participation of patients in genetic testing and the use of genetic information in medical records. Will this be enforced fully? How will it be expanded to respond to new advances?

And who has access to genetic testing? What results should be disclosed to the patient? To the family, employer, and insurer? In what manner?

With regard to health care providers, how will faith-based health care providers respond to the opportunities and challenges of precision medicine? Will abortion prohibitions be revised? Will embryonic stem cell research be more difficult to resist, especially as enormous sums of money are involved?

As you can see, advances in genetic medicine are transforming the practice of medicine. However, will a culture that insists on personal autonomy and "authenticity" be able to build ethical frameworks to guide this transformation? Will evangelical providers and faith-based medical institutions be able to work within these fields while following their religious beliefs and principles?

Other medical innovations

In addition to genetic advances that present enormous opportunities and challenges, other innovations are underway that could be ethically contentious as well.

CRISPR genetic editing

CRISPR is an acronym for Clustered Regularly Interspaced Short Palindromic Repeats. In brief, this is the name of a genetic editing technique that is revolutionizing medicine. It was used to develop techniques for detecting the presence of SARS-CoV-2, the virus that causes coronavirus. It could be used to repair defective genes causing a wide variety of maladies, including cancers and many inherited diseases.

However, it has also been used to create "designer babies." A Chinese doctor used CRISPR to engineer twin girls in 2018 so they did not have the receptor for the virus that causes AIDS. Will we see more use, or misuse, of this technology in the future?

"Three-parent babies"

Mitochondrial replacement therapy, which combines genetic material from the intended mother and father plus a female donor, can produce what is known as "three-parent babies." The procedure is currently banned in the US, but advocates claim it could help women who are carriers of serious genetic diseases to have healthy, biologically related children. However, the genetic modifications made to eggs, sperm, and embryos can be passed on to future generations. There are also safety concerns about the long-term effects on the child.

Will this technique be used in the future to customize children to their parents' specifications by using DNA from persons of unusual gifts or abilities? Will it be requested by same-sex couples who wish to create children with DNA from each parent?

Researchers have demonstrated that embryonic stem cells can be programmed to form primordial germ cells (PGCs) which can then form either eggs or sperm. As a result, PGCs could theoretically be produced from the skin of a man and turned into an egg that could be fertilized with his partner's sperm. The same procedure could turn the skin of a woman into sperm which could inseminate her partner's egg. Such techniques could produce biological children for same-sex couples.

Chimera embryos

A "chimera" is an individual composed of cells with different embryonic origins. Scientists have been creating laboratory chimeras for decades. Now, however, researchers are working on chimeras that combine human genetic material with that of animals. In April 2021, scientists announced that they had combined human stem cells with monkey embryos.

Such chimeric combinations could produce organs custom-made in an animal. For example, it is estimated that an organ grown in a pig could be prepared in as little as five months. Since the patient's DNA would be used, organ rejection could be minimized.

Chimeras could be used for drug experimentation as well. For example, human liver cells could be transplanted into a pig. Liver drugs could then be introduced and side effects monitored.

However, such research raises ethical questions regarding the appropriate use of animals for research and medical applications. Another question regards the degree to which the chimeric organization should be considered human or human cells could humanize animals. Beings could be produced that do not fully belong to either the human race or the host animal species. And the creation and/or transmission of disease across species should be considered.

In a culture that rejects absolute truth and objective ethics, how will these issues be navigated?

Cyborgs

Neil Harbisson is color-blind, but he can detect color through an antenna grafted onto his skull. As a result, he can also detect infrared and ultraviolet markings that ordinary people cannot see. Harbisson is a "cyborg." This is the abbreviated form of "cybernetic organism." From attaching bionic arms to bodies of amputation patients to creating artificial vision systems for the blind, such technology is escalating daily.

In addition to compensating for medical loss, however, cyborg advances can also enhance capacities beyond normal human abilities. Exoskeletons could enable their wearers to exceed the strength and speed of normal humans. Bionic lenses could provide capacities that far exceed normal ocular abilities. Smart contact lenses could record video by blinking. Brain-computer interfaces could enable us to communicate with the world digitally.

In a culture that prizes personal authenticity and freedom, where we will draw ethical limits around these capacities?

Physician-assisted death

"What is wonderful is that we are moving toward ways to ease suffering. We are finding legal ways for people to have the dignity of defining how they live their last days. Monumentally, this is what medicine is about at the end of life." This is how Dr. Catherine Sonquist Forest describes the legalization of "physician-assisted death" (PAD) in California. She adds: "I can't stand in judgment. These people are dying. Now, I can decide in the privacy of my office with my patient what is next."

As the push for "physician-assisted death" (PAD) continues across the country, we can expect a growing effort to force evangelical physicians doctors to provide this "service."

When the created become the creators

The rise of secularism and antagonism to biblical morality will without question affect the practice of health care and our society's approach to medical advances. Evangelical health care providers will be challenged to maintain their faith convictions if pressured by the Equality Act and similar legislation to provide services that contradict their beliefs. And scientific advances possess the capacity to redefine what it means to be human in a culture that has abandoned any biblical definition of life or consideration of God's intention for his creation.

When science fiction becomes science fact, we must act sooner than later. For all the benefits that our scientific and technological prowess promise, we must never lose sight of our moral, ethical, *biblical* calling as Christians to champion life.

To turn the tide of such a cultural upheaval, we must turn to the One who controls the winds and the waves (Matthew 8:27).

PART 3

God redeems
all he allows

Christians believe that God is all-knowing, all-powerful, and all-loving. These claims offer us our greatest hope but also open our faith to its greatest challenge.

We believe that God is all-knowing because the Bible says that God "knows everything" (1 John 3:20) and claims, "No creature is hidden from his sight, but all are naked and exposed to the eyes of him to whom we must give account" (Hebrews 4:13).

We also believe that God is all-powerful. Jesus claimed that "with God all things are possible" (Matthew 19:26). He declared: "Are not two sparrows sold for a penny? And not one of them will fall to the ground apart from your Father" (Matthew 10:29). The psalmist combined these two assertions: "Great is our Lord, and abundant in power; his understanding is beyond measure" (Psalm 147:5).

And we believe that God is all-loving. The Bible teaches that "God is love" (1 John 4:8). As a result, "God shows his love for us in that while we were still sinners, Christ died for us" (Romans 5:8).

Christians add that these three attributes are demonstrated most clearly in the life and ministry of Jesus. He knew the thoughts of those with whom he dealt (Luke 6:8; Matthew 12:25) and could predict the future (cf. Matthew 16:21); he was omnipotent over raging storms (Mark 4:35–41) and diseased bodies (cf. Matthew 8:1–4); and his love compelled his compassionate ministry (cf. Matthew 9:36).

Why, then, does he allow his people to suffer?

- Because he is omniscient, he sees the "earthquakes" we've identified in this book and their dire consequences for his people.

- Because he is omnipotent, he could stop what is happening to his people.

- Because he is all-loving, it would seem that he would want to.

And yet he has not.

I have wrestled with the theological problem of innocent suffering my entire Christian life. (I wrote extensively on the subject in *Making Sense of Suffering: 7 Biblical Ways to Help Hurting People*). I understand that much suffering comes from misused freedom (cf. Romans 1:21–32), that God can use suffering to strengthen his people (cf. 2 Corinthians 12:7–10), that we will understand the present better in the future (Romans 8:18), and that God suffers as we suffer (cf. John 11:35).

In recent years, however, I have come to embrace an additional theological truth that has given me great hope and encouragement: God redeems all he allows.

- Because he is all-knowing, he knows everything we face.

- Because he is all-powerful, he is sovereign over the world and must allow or cause all that happens.

- Because he is all-loving, his character is perfect and he can only want what is best for us.

As a result, if he allows anything he does not redeem for a greater good, he makes a mistake. But God is "holy, holy, holy" and cannot make a mistake (Isaiah 6:3; Revelation 4:8).

Therefore, he must redeem all he allows.

I am not suggesting that we will see or understand such redemption in this life. I don't understand the airplanes on which I fly or the computer on which I am typing these words. But one day we will understand what we do not understand today (1 Corinthians 13:12) and see how "for those who love God all things work together for good" (Romans 8:28).

In the meantime, our Father calls us to join him in redeeming the tsunami we are facing. Rather than retreating from the challenges we face, let's embrace them. Rather than withdrawing from the culture, keeping our salt in the saltshaker and our light under a basket (Matthew 5:13–16), let's engage those who oppose biblical morality by "speaking the truth in love" (Ephesians 4:15).

In this concluding part, we'll discover ways to defend biblical truth with persuasive clarity and personal compassion. And we'll find ways to turn our obstacles into opportunities and our challenges into open doors for the gospel.

Our Lord is calling us to partner with him in redeeming these days for his glory and our good.

It is always too soon to give up on God.

"Don't ever take a fence down until you know why it was put up."
—**ROBERT FROST**

9

Defending biblical truth with reason and relevance

In chapter 1 we discussed the postmodern attack on truth. If all truth claims are personal and subjective, biblical truth claims are personal and subjective as well. In our culture, the Bible is no more intrinsically authoritative than the Book of Mormon, the Qur'an, or your personal diary. Your truth is your truth and my truth is my truth, or so we're told.

If we cannot defend objective truth and biblical authority, we lose a significant part of the foundation for our worldview, our faith, and our mission in our fallen world. As a result, it is essential that Christians be able to respond to the attack on truth with clarity and persuasive effectiveness.

I have taught entire semesters in seminaries on what follows. For our purposes, I'll shorten a very long discussion into some key points. What follows is not all we *could* know about defending truth and biblical authority, but what we *need* to know today.

How to defend truth

The claim that objective truth is unknowable is not new. A philosophical movement appropriately known as Skepticism arose more than three centuries before Christ. Following Pyrrho (c. 365 to 270 BC), this movement was prominent from the first century before Christ to the second and third centuries of the Christian era.

From then until now, skeptics have argued that truth is either unknowable by definition or unknowable by humans. This is a kind of agnosticism (from the Greek *a*, meaning "not," and *gnosis*, meaning "knowledge"). Applied to God, "hard" agnostics claim that the existence of God cannot be known; "soft" agnostics claim that they are uncertain about whether he exists or not. Many take these approaches to the existence of objective truth as well.

However, the postmodern rejection of truth fails in at least three ways.

Logical issues

To claim that there is no such thing as absolute truth is to make an absolute truth claim. This is like saying, "There's no such thing as certainty, and we're certain of it." The next time someone tells you that "their truth" is true for them, ask them why you should believe them. After all, it can be "your truth" that "their truth" is false. Doctors must sometimes convince patients that their disease is more serious than they want to believe it to be. If the patient claims that "their truth" is "the truth," they are admitting that "the truth" exists.

The fact that we are having this discussion points to the fact of objective truth. Otherwise, every word I have written could mean whatever I or you want it to mean.

Philosopher R. J. Snell is right: "Just as one cannot deny the principle of non-contradiction without utilizing that very principle, so one cannot deny our ability to know the truth without making truth claims and—by that very act—affirming the possibility and necessity of truth."

An apologist was holding a discussion with a group of college students when one of them stated, "I don't believe that we are living in a coherent universe." The apologist replied, "Would you like my answer to be coherent or not?"

To deny that objective truth exists requires the existence of objective truth.

Moral issues

If "all truth is personal," then all moral claims are equally subjective and personal. In this case, we have no objective basis to critique the ethics of others, no matter how abhorrent we find them to be.

In the years following 9/11, I spent a good deal of time studying radical jihadists and their beliefs. When I was in college, I lived for a time in the Muslim world; I have taught world religions on four seminary faculties and have read and studied the Qur'an. However, I had not encountered the ideology that drove terrorists to fly planes into buildings. What I discovered was that a very cohesive worldview motivated them and others committed to their jihadist movement.

An Islamic scholar named Sayyid Qutb, writing in the 1960s, argued that the "golden age" of Islam (the first century following the Prophet Muhammad) was true Islam. He believed that the Muslim world had deviated drastically from its theological and moral roots and wanted to persuade Muslims to return to their "pure" origins. In his view, the Muslim governments then in place around the world were far too secular and too compromised with the non-Muslim world. As a result, "true" Muslims must overthrow these governments and those who support them.

In addition, some in the Muslim world came to interpret the Qur'an (especially Surah 2:190–191) to teach that they must attack all peoples who have (in their opinion) attacked Islam. Since they consider the founding of Israel in 1948 to be a theft of land from its rightful Muslim owners, they see Israel as an enemy that must be attacked in order to defend Islam. Since the US supports Israel, we are complicit in this attack, in their view.

One other element: Osama bin Laden and others claimed that democracy is heresy since we have the "pure" teachings of Allah in the Qur'an. In addition, those living in democracies elect their leaders and support their militaries through their taxes and personal engagement. As a result, bin Laden claimed, there are no "innocent" victims in America and the West. You and I are complicit in this attack on Islam, which must be repudiated so the Muslim world can be purified and return to its founding path.

All of this explains why nineteen "terrorists" (they would have called themselves "martyrs") attacked America on 9/11. They would have said that they were not attacking "innocent" Americans but defending Islam from its imperialistic, crusading enemies. They attacked the Twin Towers (representing financial power), the Pentagon (the military), and probably intended to attack the White House or Congress (the political), all to prove that the powers of the West can be defeated by the forces of Islam.

Of course, you and I (along with most of the Muslim world) would reject every element of this ideology. My purpose is not to agree with it but to point out that for the 9/11 terrorists, this was "their truth."

If all truth is personal, what right do we have to reject their moral truth?

We could make the same argument with regard to the Holocaust or the epidemic of mass shootings in recent years. In each case, a person's moral "truth" is "their truth."

We can respond, of course, with the assertion that people have no right to personal truth that harms others. However, on what logical basis can we make this assertion? And how do we define "harms others"? If the content of this book offends even one person, do I then have a right to believe and promote its contents?

We could assert that truth claims that accomplish the greatest good for the greatest number of people are therefore valid (the utilitarian approach). But what of the rights of the minority?

As you can see, relative truth can lead to horrific moral claims and consequences.

Practical issues

Imagine trying to live consistently by relative truth.

- Traffic regulations are to be obeyed only if they are "your truth."

- The laws of your society are to be followed only if you agree with them personally.

- Students can study whatever they want, as they want, when they want.

- Doctors are to be believed only if their diagnosis aligns with yours.

- Bankers' statements regarding the amount of your money in their accounts are only their opinions; yours are just as valid.

- People are as old as they say they are whether their birth certificate agrees or not.

These are fallacious possibilities, to be sure. But why are they less logical than the following?

- You are the gender you believe yourself to be regardless of your anatomy and the sex "assigned" to you at birth.

- If you are pregnant, your fetus will experience the medical and legal protections afforded by America to you only if you consider him or her to be a person. Otherwise, based on your opinion, his or her life can be ended legally.

- You deserve the help of doctors in ending your life whether you are suffering from terminal medical conditions or not.

- You can choose euthanasia for relatives if you believe that their lives no longer possess inherent meaning or value. Missionaries in Belgium have told me that in their country, families are making such arrangements for their elderly relatives without their relatives' consent.

Both lists are logical and practical consequences of abandoning objective truth.

It is clear that objective truth must exist even for us to have the capacity to discuss its existence. So, let's consider a second question: Which truth? Are there objective reasons to claim that the Bible is true and trustworthy?

How to defend biblical truth

The question came from nowhere. I was leading a youth Bible study when a high school freshman asked me, "How do you know the Bible came from God?" The look in his eyes showed how serious he was. His father was a Sunday school teacher and leader in our church, but that wasn't good enough. Nor should it have been.

A few days later, a friend and I got into a discussion about my faith and he asked, "Why do you trust the Bible? After all those centuries of copying, surely you don't think you have what was first written. How can you trust it today?"

The Bible says of itself:

- "All Scripture is breathed out by God and profitable for teaching, for reproof, for correction, and for training in righteousness, that the man of God may be complete, equipped for every good work" (2 Timothy 3:16–17).

- Paul claimed that his message was received "through a revelation of Jesus Christ" (Galatians 1:12).

- Peter asserted that the authors of Scripture "spoke from God as they were carried along by the Holy Spirit" (2 Peter 1:21).

- The prophet proclaimed, "The grass withers, the flower fades, but the word of our God will stand forever" (Isaiah 40:8).

However, you would expect the Bible and its proponents to make these claims. Muslims believe the Qur'an to be the direct revelation of Allah through the Prophet Muhammad. Buddhists and Hindus believe their sacred writings to be sacred writings. As we saw earlier in this chapter, claiming something to be true doesn't make it true. Is there objective evidence that the Bible is the true and trustworthy word of God?

Archaeological evidence for the Bible

We have excellent archaeological data to support the rest of the biblical witness. Here are some examples, listed in the order of their biblical occurrence.

Old Testament discoveries

Archaeologists working with the ruins of Jericho made this astounding discovery in the 1930s: the walls fell outward. Typically, attackers used poles and rams to push stone walls inward. In this case, they fell down and out, making it easy for the Israelites to climb them and take the city (Joshua 6:20).

In 1993, Israeli archaeologists were sifting through debris as they worked on the ruins of the ancient city of Dan in upper Galilee. What they discovered that day would make the front page of the *New York Times*: an inscription, part of a shattered "stele" (monument) and dated to the ninth century before Christ. It commemorated a military victory by the king of Damascus over the king of Israel and the house of David. And it cited the "House of David" clearly and without question.

This was the first non-biblical artifact proving the existence of the great King of Israel. A year later, two other artifacts were discovered naming Jehoram, king of Israel, and Ahaziah, king of Judah. Many scholars now believe that the monument naming them relates to the battle in the region recorded in 2 Chronicles 22:5.

Archaeologists have also discovered dramatic evidence of Solomon's amazing wealth and building campaigns. Fortifications at Hazor, Megiddo, and Gezer date to the middle of the tenth century BC, exactly the time of Solomon's reign. Solomon's "Royal Quarter" has been unearthed in Jerusalem. And part of the Temple he built still stands on the eastern side of the Temple Mount.

Babylonian chronicles of the destruction of Jerusalem parallel precisely the biblical records of this tragic event. And ruins of Nebuchadnezzar's palace complex have been discovered, proving his existence and significant role in the ancient Middle East.

New Testament evidence

According to Luke 3:1, Lysanias was tetrarch of Abilene during the beginning of John the Baptist's ministry. But no evidence of Lysanius's existence had been discovered until an inscription was found which records a temple dedication by him. His name, title, and place all agree with Luke's description.

In 1990, workers building a water park two miles south of the Temple Mount inadvertently broke through the ceiling of a hidden burial chamber. Archaeologists found twelve limestone ossuaries inside. One of them, decorated with six-petaled rosettes, contained the bones of a sixty-year-old man, and it bore the inscription *Yehosef bar Qayafa*, "Joseph son of Caiaphas." Historians have identified the remains as those of the high priest of Jesus' execution.

In 1961, excavations at the seaside ruins of Caesarea Maritima unearthed a first-century inscription. Badly damaged, the Latin inscription reads in part, *Tiberieum . . . [Pon]tius Pilatus . . . [Praef] ectus Juda[ea]e*. The inscription confirms the status of Pontius Pilate as the prefect or governor of Judea.

Yohanan Yehohanan was a crucifixion victim who was executed during the Jewish Revolt in AD 70. In 1968, his remains were discovered. His legs were fractured, evidence of the typical Roman means by which death was hastened. Nails were driven through his wrists and heels. His death corresponds precisely with the descriptions of Jesus' crucifixion found in the Gospels (cf. John 19:17–32).

Luke describes Paul's ministry in Corinth and this event: "When Gallio was proconsul of Achaia, the Jews made a united attack on Paul" (Acts 18:12). Gallio ejected Paul's accusers from his court (v. 16) and refused to prosecute Paul. This Gallio is known to be the brother of Seneca, the philosopher, who was himself tutor of Nero. However, critics were skeptical of Luke's claim that Gallio was "proconsul" of Achaia during the time of Paul's ministry there.

Then an inscription was discovered at Delphi with this exact title for Gallio; it dates him to AD 51, the time Paul was in Corinth.

Erastus is identified in Acts 19:22 as one of Paul's Corinthian coworkers. In excavations in the area of Corinth, we find an inscription which states, "Erastus in return for his aedileship laid the pavement at his own expense."

Fulfilled prophecy

Jeane Dixon made the news after President Kennedy's assassination when her prediction reported four years earlier in *Parade* magazine was recounted: "As to the 1960 election, Mrs. Dixon thinks it will be dominated by labor and won by a Democrat. But he will be assassinated or die in office, though not necessarily in his first term."

However, in January of 1960, she had claimed, "The symbol of the Presidency is directly over the head of Vice President Nixon." Either he or Democrat John Kennedy had to win the election. Additionally, three of the ten presidents who served in the twentieth century had died in office, and two others were critically ill at the end of their term. The odds against her were not as high as we might think.

Further study of psychic claims made in 1975 and observed until 1981 concluded that only six of the seventy-two predictions were fulfilled in any way. An 8 percent accuracy rate is not impressive.

By contrast, does the Bible fulfill its predictions? When it makes prophetic statements regarding the future, do they come to pass? As we consider the evidence for biblical authority, we should spend a moment with the fascinating subject of messianic prophecy and its fulfillment by Jesus Christ. If any book makes promises it does not keep, we are justified in dismissing the rest of its truth claims. But if a book's prophecies rendered centuries earlier are clearly fulfilled in history, we can consider the rest of its claims to be trustworthy as well.

The importance of Messianic prophecy

Jesus appealed repeatedly to Old Testament predictions regarding himself:

- At the beginning of his ministry, he read a Messianic prediction from Isaiah 61, then said to the waiting crowd, "Today this Scripture has been fulfilled in your hearing" (Luke 4:21).

- He told his critics, "You search the Scriptures because you think that in them you have eternal life; and it is they that bear witness about me, yet you refuse to come to me that you may have life. . . . For if you believed Moses, you would believe me; for he wrote of me" (John 5:39–40, 46).

- At the Last Supper, he warned his disciples, "For I tell you that this Scripture must be fulfilled in me: 'And he was numbered with the transgressors.' For what is written about me has its fulfillment" (Luke 22:37).

- At his arrest, he told the crowd, "All this has taken place that the Scriptures of the prophets might be fulfilled" (Matthew 26:56).

- On Easter Sunday night, he said to the two disciples traveling to Emmaus: "O foolish ones, and slow of heart to believe all that the prophets have spoken! Was it not necessary that the Christ should suffer these things and enter into his glory?" Then, to explain what he meant, "beginning with Moses and all the Prophets, he interpreted to them in all the Scriptures the things concerning himself" (Luke 24:25–26, 27).

- After his resurrection, he said to his astonished disciples, "Everything written about me in the Law of Moses and the Prophets and the Psalms must be fulfilled" (Luke 24:44).

New Testament writers made the same appeal, claiming repeatedly that Jesus fulfilled the Old Testament predictions regarding the Messiah:

- At Pentecost, Peter cited prophecies from Joel 2, Psalm 16, and Psalm 110 in claiming that Jesus was the promised Messiah (Acts 2:14–36).

- He later explained Jesus' crucifixion to a crowd at Jerusalem: "What God foretold by the mouth of all the prophets, that his Christ would suffer, he thus fulfilled" (Acts 3:18).

- Peter told Cornelius, "To him all the prophets bear witness that everyone who believes in him receives forgiveness of sins through his name" (Acts 19:43).

- When Paul came to Thessalonica, "[He] went in, as was his custom, and on three Sabbath days he reasoned with them from the Scriptures, explaining and proving that it was necessary for the Christ to suffer and to rise from the dead, and saying, 'This Jesus, whom I proclaim to you, is the Christ'" (Acts 17:2–3).

- Paul described his message as "[The gospel of God] which he promised beforehand through his prophets in the holy Scriptures" (Romans 1:2).

- Paul's message could be summarized: "Christ died for our sins in accordance with the Scriptures, that he was buried, that he was raised on the third day in accordance with the Scriptures" (1 Corinthians 15:3–4).

Clearly, if Jesus did not fulfill Old Testament predictions regarding the Messiah, both he and his first followers were deceivers of the worst sort. Their movement depended entirely on the claim that he was the promised Messiah of God. It still does.

Representative Messianic prophecies

More than three hundred times, the Old Testament makes claims or predictions regarding the coming Messiah. Jesus fulfilled every one of them. Most scholars date Malachi, the last book of the Old Testament, at circa 400 BC, demonstrating that these predictions were not made during Jesus' day. Translators who created the Septuagint, the Greek Old Testament, began their work around 250 BC. At the very least, the prophecies they translated were made more than two centuries between the last prediction and Jesus' fulfillment of those prophecies.

Listed in order relative to Jesus' earthly life, here are some of the main prophecies to consider:

- Born of a woman's seed (Genesis 3:15; Galatians 4:4)

- Born of a virgin (Isaiah 7:14; Matthew 1:18, 24, 25; Luke 1:26–35)

- Descended from Abraham (Genesis 22:18; Matthew 1:1; Galatians 3:16)

- Descended from Isaac (Genesis 21:12; Luke 3:23, 34; Matthew 1:2)

- Descended from Jacob (Numbers 24:17; Luke 3:23, 34)

- Part of the tribe of Judah (Genesis 49:19; Micah 5:2; Luke 3:23, 33; Matthew 1:2)

- From the family line of Jesse (Isaiah 11:1; Luke 3:23, 32; Matthew 1:6)

- From the house of David (Jeremiah 23:5; Luke 3:23, 31; Matthew 1:1)

- Born at Bethlehem (Micah 5:2; Matthew 2:1)

- Presented with gifts (Psalm 72:10; Matthew 2:1, 11)

- Children would die (Jeremiah 31:15; Matthew 2:16)

- Would be anointed by the Spirit (Isaiah 11:2; Matthew 3:16, 17)

- Preceded by a messenger (Isaiah 40:3; Malachi 3:1; Matthew 3:1, 2)

- Would minister in Galilee (Isaiah 9:1; Matthew 4:12, 13, 17)

- Would perform miracles (Isaiah 35:5, 6; Matthew 9:35)

- Would teach parables (Psalm 78:2; Matthew 13:34)

- Would enter Jerusalem on a donkey (Zechariah 9:9; Luke 19:35–37)

- A friend would betray him (Psalm 41:9; Matthew 10:4)

- Sold for thirty pieces of silver (Zechariah 11:12; Matthew 26:15)

- Money thrown in the Lord's house (Zechariah 11:13; Matthew 27:5)

- Money used for a potter's field (Zechariah 11:13; Matthew 27:7)

- Forsaken by his disciples (Zechariah 13:7; Mark 14:50)

- Accused by false witnesses (Psalm 35:11; Matthew 26:59, 60)

- Silent before his accusers (Isaiah 53:7; Matthew 27:12)

- Wounded and bruised (Isaiah 53:5; Matthew 27:26)

- Smitten and spit upon (Isaiah 50:6; Matthew 26:67)

- Mocked (Psalm 22:7, 8; Matthew 27:29)

- Hands and feet pierced (Psalm 22:16; Luke 23:33)

- Crucified with thieves (Isaiah 53:12; Matthew 27:38)

- Prayed for his persecutors (Isaiah 53:12; Luke 23:34)

- Friends stood afar off (Psalm 38:11; Luke 23:49)

- Garments parted and lots cast (Psalm 22:18; John 19:23, 24)

- Would suffer thirst (Psalm 69:21; John 19:28)

- Gall and vinegar offered (Psalm 69:2; Matthew 27:34)

- Would be forsaken by God (Psalm 22:1; Matthew 27:46)

- Would commit himself to God (Psalm 31:5; Luke 23:46)

- No bones broken (Psalm 34:20; John 19:33)

- His side pierced (Zechariah 12:10; John 19:34)

- Buried in a wealthy man's tomb (Isaiah 53:9; Matthew 27:57–60)

- Would be raised from the dead (Psalm 16:10; Acts 2:31)

- Would ascend to heaven (Psalm 68:18; Acts 1:9)

- Would be seated at the right hand of God (Psalm 110:1; Hebrews 1:3)

What are the chances that one person could fulfill each of these predictions?

Many of them were beyond Jesus' human control (such as the soldier's decision to thrust his spear into Jesus' side). Were they coincidental? Mathematician Peter Stoner once calculated the odds of one man's fulfillment of just eight of these predictions: one in ten to the seventeenth power (one followed by seventeen zeroes). That number would fill the state of Texas two feet deep in silver dollars. Stoner then considered forty-eight of the Messianic prophecies and determined the odds of fulfilling them to be one in ten to the 157th power.

Clearly, the Bible keeps its promises. And its central figure is who he claimed to be: the Messiah of God.

Redeeming the attack on biblical truth

I began teaching Christian apologetics (methods of defending the faith) in a day when postmodern relativism was only beginning to become popular across our culture. Accordingly, I taught my students how to use rational, empirical, and evidential arguments to defend the Bible, the existence of God, the resurrection and deity of Jesus, and other central doctrines.

Today, if I make such arguments with those who have adopted postmodern relativism, they are likely to reply, "That's just your truth." Even the archaeological and prophetic evidence we have discussed in this chapter can be dismissed by those who dismiss all objective evidence.

As a result, when defending our faith and freedom, it is important to begin at the beginning. If we lose the debate over the existence of truth, it is difficult to persuade our culture that its other assumptions are false. The first section of this chapter is intended to help us win that debate so that we can then win the debate over the truthfulness of God's word.

However, in a postmodern culture, your most powerful argument is your changed life. When people see the difference Jesus makes in your life, they may be drawn to seek such a difference in their lives.

Remember the man born blind who was healed by Jesus (John 9). When asked to account for his healing, he testified: "One thing I do know, that though I was blind, now I see" (v. 25).

Your story will touch hearts whose minds may be closed to truth. If you and I will think and live biblically, the results will become obvious in our lives. Then, as we engage our culture over *my* truth and *the* truth, they'll see how the former was transformed by the latter and will be drawn to the One who *is* the truth (John 14:6).

This is how I came to faith in Jesus. As I stated in the introduction to this book, I grew up in a home with no spiritual life but all my father's spiritual questions: Why does God allow innocent suffering? What about science and faith? World religions?

When I was invited to church for the first time as a teenager, I was not led to Christ through the doctrinal brilliance of the pastor (though he was an outstanding communicator) or the theological sophistication of my Bible teacher (though she was a gifted teacher). Rather, I saw something in the other teenagers I did not see in myself. I sensed a purpose, joy, and fellowship I had never encountered before.

On September 9, 1973, I asked my Bible study teacher how I could have what they had, and she led me to faith in Jesus.

What happened for me has happened for billions of people across Christian history. This is because Jesus is still Lord and his love still transforms those who give themselves to him. He still makes us a "new creation" (2 Corinthians 5:17). All he has ever done, he can still do.

When we focus on Jesus with our lives and our witness, like John the Baptist, we decrease that our Lord might increase (John 3:30). We lead people from ourselves to our Savior. And our attitudes, words, and lives show his relevance and power even in our secularized culture.

Let's redeem the battle for truth by demonstrating the relevance of God's truth in our lives and our joy. We cannot measure the eternal significance of present faithfulness.

"The difference between man and woman is not meant to stand in opposition, or to subordinate, but is for the sake of communion and generation, always in the image and likeness of God." —POPE FRANCIS

10

Defending biblical sexuality with grace and truth

We are all broken sexually. Heterosexual lust is sinful (Matthew 5:28), just as homosexual lust is sinful. In the churches I led we had several problems with heterosexual moral failure among our staff, but never one involving homosexual moral failure. I say this to say that biblical sexuality is holistic. It speaks to the whole of the human condition and experience, calling each and every one of us to lives God can bless.

In chapter 2, we discussed the sexual revolution and its tragic assault on biblical morality. In this chapter, we'll survey some practical ways to defend God's plan for our lives and sexuality. Then we'll focus on ways to redeem this controversy for the sake of our broken culture and broken lives.

The Bible and homosexuality

We'll begin at the beginning: the Bible clearly and consistently forbids same-sex sexual relationships. It prohibits such activity in the Old Testament (Leviticus 18:22; 20:13) and the New Testament (Romans 1:26–27; 1 Corinthians 6:9–10; 1 Timothy 1:8–11).

Is the Bible wrong?

As we have noted, some LGBTQ advocates claim that the Bible is simply wrong or outdated in these assertions. They typically cite slavery as a topic where the Bible is clearly wrong; in their view, it is just as wrong on LGBTQ issues.

In response, let's consider four historical facts.

One: Slavery was a global fact in the ancient world. Nonetheless, the Old Testament provided a way for slaves to be freed (Exodus 21:8), especially if they were injured by their masters (v. 26). Hebrews were to be held as slaves no longer than six years (Deuteronomy 15:12); the Jubilee Year, which occurred every forty-nine years, freed all Israelite slaves (Leviticus 25:50).

Two: Christians had no legal or political power to end slavery in the Roman Empire, but they abolished even the possibility of racial or social discrimination for followers of Jesus: "There is neither Jew nor Greek, there is neither slave nor free, there is no male and female, for you are all one in Christ Jesus" (Galatians 3:28). Paul appealed to Philemon to free his slave Onesimus (Philemon 16).

Three: The New Testament church gave those who were enslaved a family and a home. This was one reason why so many of the earliest believers were slaves. Pastors and congregational leaders were drawn from the ranks both of slaves and free. Christians made no distinction between the two, for their Father welcomed all as his children.

Four: Not a single New Testament leader owned slaves or condoned such, even though many had the means to purchase them (cf. Nicodemus, Joseph of Arimathea, and Barnabas). Their example inspired William Wilberforce and countless other Christians to do all they could to abolish slavery, and we thank God that they were successful.

The Bible was not wrong on slavery, just as it is not wrong on LGBTQ issues.

Are we wrong?

As we have noted, some interpreters claim that we are misinterpreting the biblical texts. In their view, the Bible never addresses monogamous, loving, consensual same-sex relationships. It forbids sexual abuse, not loving sexual expression.

Such interpreters point to those who used the Bible to advocate for slavery in the pre-Civil War era. If the Bible does not condone slavery, as we have seen, such advocates misinterpreted it to advance their own oppressive ends. In the view of some, interpreters like me are doing the same with regard to LGBTQ issues today. This approach is appealing to many since it seems to offer a way to affirm both the Bible and LGBTQ behavior.

Since Matthew Vines and David Gushee have written popular books encapsulating this argument, we will consider their claims as representative.

Matthew Vines

Matthew Vines is the author of *God and the Gay Christian: The Biblical Case in Support of Same-Sex Relationships*. Vines was a philosophy student at Harvard before leaving school to pursue a full-time study of the biblical statements regarding homosexuality.

He says of himself, "Like most theologically conservative Christians, I hold what is often called a 'high view' of the Bible. That means I believe all of Scripture is inspired by God and authoritative for my life." At the same time, Vines is convinced that homosexual orientation and behavior are not sinful. As a gay Christian, he seeks to reconcile his experience with God's word.

A summary of his argument:

- We can tell truth by its "fruit" (Matthew 7:15–20). Forbidding homosexual behavior damages those with same-sex attraction, but celibacy is untenable for most gay people. Thus the "fruit" of rejecting same-sex behavior shows such prohibition to be wrong.

- The Scriptures know nothing of same-sex orientation, only behavior. They forbid same-sex behavior in excess but do not address monogamous, loving same-sex relationships. Early Christians shared this ignorance of homosexual orientation.

- The "sin of Sodom" was not homosexuality but attempted gang rape.

- Leviticus prohibits homosexual relations because the ancient world viewed them as denigrating or feminizing the passive partner. Since we no longer view such relations in this way, these prohibitions are no longer relevant to our culture.

- In the Greco-Roman context, Romans 1 warns against heterosexual men who oppress and denigrate other men through same-sex acts, not partners in a consensual, loving relationship.

- Paul's use of *arsenokoites* (translated by the ESV as "men who practice homosexuality" in 1 Corinthians 6:9

and 1 Timothy 1:10) refers to economic exploitation, not sexual behavior.

- God's covenant expectation for marriage can be fulfilled by homosexuals living in a monogamous, faithful relationship.

The same week Vines published his book, the faculty of Southern Baptist Theological Seminary released an e-book, *God and the Gay Christian? A Response to Matthew Vines*. Edited by seminary president Albert Mohler, its authors deal with each of Vines's proposals in turn.

A summary of their responses:

- The sin of Sodom is described in Ezekiel 16:50 as an "abomination," using the singular form of the Hebrew term *toevah*. This term is used in the singular only twice in Leviticus, when it calls same-sex intercourse an "abomination" (Leviticus 18:22) and prescribes the death penalty for it (Leviticus 20:13). Thus, we should view the sin of Sodom as we do the sin referenced in Leviticus: same-sex relations.

- If Vines is right about Leviticus, only the stronger partner denigrating the weaker should be punished. But in the biblical text, both are to be punished equally.

- Romans was written to Jewish Christians and should be interpreted in a Jewish context, not a Roman one.

- Romans 1 forbids "men committing shameless acts with men" (v. 27), which shows that both men were active in this relationship. Thus, Vines is wrong to interpret the text as referring to a man denigrating an unwilling partner.

- Other words for homosexual behavior were available to Paul, but he coined *arsenokoites*, a term that derives from the Greek translation of Leviticus 20:13, *arsenos koiten*. Clearly, he had the Levitical prohibition in mind.

- Contrary to Vines's claim, early Christians such as Tertullian, Chrysostom, and Ambrosiaster clearly warned against homosexual passion.

- Vines claims that the Bible knows nothing of homosexual "orientation" since it does not use this word. However, it uses the synonym "desire" (2 Peter 3:3; Jude 16; Romans 13:14; Galatians 5:16; James 1:14).

- If Scripture is ignorant about homosexual orientation, where else is God's word ignorant about human nature? Why did God inspire a text that would mislead the world for twenty centuries? What does this supposed ignorance say about God's remedy for sin through the atonement of Christ?

Mohler states: "Biblical Christianity can neither endorse same-sex marriage nor accept the claim that a believer can be obedient to Christ and remain or persist in same-sex behaviors. The church is the assembly of the redeemed, saved from our sins and learning obedience in the school of Christ. Every single one of us is a sexual sinner in need of redemption, but we are called to holiness, to obedience, and to honoring marriage as one of God's most precious gifts and as a picture of the relationship between Christ and the church."

He then concludes: "The church has often failed people with same-sex attractions and failed them horribly. We must not fail them now by forfeiting the only message that leads to salvation, holiness, and faithfulness."

David Gushee

Dr. David Gushee teaches ethics at Mercer University, a Baptist school in Georgia. Recognized as a leading Christian ethicist, his announcement in 2014 that he now supports covenanted same-sex relationships shocked many.

His book *Changing Our Mind* tells the story of his decision. Gushee's sister came out as a lesbian in 2008. In the following years, he developed an increasing number of personal relationships with gay Christians and began to grieve for the rejection they had experienced from Christians and churches. In 2012, he co-hosted a conference on sexual ethics during which he was moved by the stories of "deeply-hurt-by-the-church-but-still-committed-to-Jesus-gay Christians." His own experiences as a bullied teenager caused him to resonate with their pain, as did his doctoral studies on the Holocaust.

Gushee's book invites those who affirm what he calls the "traditional" position on same-sex relations to reconsider their interpretation of Scripture. He describes the arguments proposed by those who affirm such reinterpretation but offers no new insights on biblical texts himself.

His shift turns on three proposals:

- Old Testament creation narratives are theological accounts, not scientific descriptions. As we learn more about human nature (e.g., the existence of unchanging same-sex orientation), we are free to modify our application of these narratives. Just as we shifted from an earth-centric to a helio-centric understanding of our galaxy, so we can shift our understanding of sexual orientation without violating Scripture.

- We should not rely on arguments from God's purported design for humans since such arguments have been "remarkably problematic" across Christian history. For instance, Christians have been wrong to cite human dominion in rejecting environmental concerns or to cite Genesis 9's "curse of Ham" in supporting slavery. In the same way, we are wrong to discriminate against gay people on the basis of Genesis narratives.

- We live in a "Genesis 3" world where everyone is flawed and broken sexually, not just those of same-sex attraction. Thus, we should offer grace with humility.

My responses:

- Gushee's first proposal opens us to the charge that the Bible is wrong or misinformed on the human condition. If this is true regarding same-sex attraction, where else is it true? Polyamory? Consensual sexual relations of any kind with people or even animals?

- His second proposal commits the "genetic fallacy," rejecting an idea because of its source rather than its merit. The argument that humans were intended only for opposite-sex erotic relationships originates in Genesis narratives (which he claims have been widely misinterpreted). As a result, he believes that argument should be questioned.

- His third proposal is by far his strongest, in my view. Gushee is right: we are all broken and flawed sexually. However, this fact does not mean we should affirm what the Bible forbids. To do so denies gay Christians the very truth that can most liberate them.

His larger argument commits the "bandwagon" fallacy, claiming that the growing popularity of his position is a reason to accept it. And he commits a logical *non sequitur* ("it does not follow") when he states that Christians have been wrong on slavery, the Jews, and women's rights, so we must be wrong on homosexuality. In fact, as we will see in the next chapter, the historical record shows that slavery was never accepted or defended by the majority of Christians. By contrast, until recently the Christian church unanimously viewed homosexual activity as forbidden by Scripture.

However, Gushee is very helpful when he insists that all sexual relationships should be covenantal in nature. Rejecting the "mutual consent ethic" and the "loving relationship ethic," he affirms the "covenantal-marital sexual ethical standard—one person, for life, faithful and exclusive, in a loving, nonexploitative, noncoercive, reciprocal relationship, that is the highest expression of biblical sexual ethics."

Note that both Vines and Gushee came to their interpretation of Scripture regarding same-sex marriage out of personal biases in favor of same-sex relations. We should always beware of interpreting God's word through the prism of personal experience. Rather, we should interpret experience by divine revelation.

The Bible and premarital sex

The Bachelorette debuted in 2003. A single bachelorette decides between a pool of bachelors; to date, three of the sixteen seasons have resulted in marriages between the bachelorette and the person she chose.

Katie Thurston, the bachelorette for the season that debuted in June 2021, made headlines because of what she called her "sex positivity." She explained that "I talk about sex in a very casual way" and refers to sexual activities I will not describe here. She said fans will see "some conversations" around sex positivity "because it is 2021 and it's important we talk about it, especially with our partners."

According to a therapist interviewed in the *yahoo!* article on Thurston's announcement, "Being nonjudgmental is at the heart of sex positivity." Another therapist stated that this is an especially important conversation now, given that sex is still often viewed "as a sin." She added: "This can be a good move for this franchise to start the dialogue publicly on healthy sexuality. It can be the swing we need as a culture."

A third therapist added that we should "support and show reverence to sex workers, who provide essential services." Otherwise, she warned, "sex positivity" is "selective sexual freedom that is often self-serving."

As we have noted, the sexual revolution promoted a new ethic not just with regard to LGBTQ activity but with many other sexual activities as well, including premarital sex, adultery, pornography, and prostitution. Are there objective, nonreligious ways to defend biblical morality from this onslaught?

God's intention for sex

The God who created us made us sexual beings. He designed us in such a way that "it is not good that the man should be alone" (Genesis 2:18a). As a result, the Lord made "a helper fit for him" (v. 18b). God intended sex to be a celebration of their intimacy and the means by which they would "be fruitful and multiply" (Genesis 1:28).

From then until now, God's intention for sex is clear: "A man shall leave his father and his mother and hold fast to his wife, and they shall become one flesh" (Genesis 2:24). When Jesus was asked by the Pharisees about divorce, he quoted this verse and added, "They are no longer two but one flesh. What therefore God has joined together, let not man separate" (Matthew 19:5–6).

As a result, God's word forbids sex outside of marriage: "You shall not commit adultery" (Exodus 20:14); "Let marriage be held in honor among all, and let the marriage bed be undefiled" (Hebrews 13:4). His word also forbids sex before marriage (1 Corinthians 7:1–2) and all other sexual immorality (1 Corinthians 6:18; 1 Thessalonians 4:3), including lust (Matthew 5:28).

Consequences of premarital sex

Sixty-nine percent of Americans say sex between an unmarried man and woman is morally acceptable, up sixteen points since 2002. In addition, 42 percent believe sex between teenagers is morally acceptable.

However, we should note: Since this revolution began in the 1960s, the youth suicide rate is the highest it has been since the government began collecting such data in 1960. The percentage of children born out of wedlock has escalated from 8 percent in 1962 to 40 percent today. The odds that children in single-parent homes will live in poverty are high.

Sexually transmitted diseases (STDs) are another consequence of sex outside of marriage. If people remained virgins until marriage and remained faithful to their spouses in marriage, there would obviously be no such diseases. The fact that, at this writing, STDs have reached all-time highs for six consecutive years in the US points to the medical consequences of rejecting God's plan for sex.

Such consequences extend not only to those who engage in unbiblical sexual activity but to the babies such activity can produce. At this writing, more than sixty-two million babies have been killed by abortion since *Roe v. Wade*. This tragic fact is relevant to our discussion since 86 percent of abortions are obtained by unmarried women. And it leads us to our next section.

The Bible and abortion

The most disastrous consequence of the sexual revolution's attack on biblical morality has been its consequences for unborn babies.

Since the Supreme Court legalized abortion in 1973, the number of babies who have died by abortion exceeds the populations of Kentucky, Oregon, Oklahoma, Connecticut, Iowa, Mississippi, Arkansas, Kansas, Utah, Nevada, New Mexico, West Virginia,

Nebraska, Idaho, Maine, New Hampshire, Hawaii, Rhode Island, Montana, Delaware, South Dakota, Alaska, North Dakota, Vermont, and Wyoming—*combined*. Abortion is the leading cause of death in America, surpassing heart disease, cancer, and all other causes.

Let's consider arguments for abortion made by its advocates, then discuss ways to counter them.

Moral arguments for abortion

"Pro-choice" advocates make five basic claims:

1. No one can say when a fetus becomes a person, so the mother is the most appropriate person to make decisions regarding it.

2. Abortion must be protected so a woman who is the victim of rape or incest does not have to bear a child resulting from such an attack.

3. No unwanted child should be brought into the world.

4. The state has no right to legislate personal morality.

5. A woman must be permitted to make pregnancy decisions in light of her life circumstances.

Many theologians, pastors, and denominational leaders consider these claims to be both biblical and moral.

First, "pro-choice" proponents argue that a fetus is not legally a "person." They agree with the Supreme Court's finding that the Constitution nowhere grants legal standing to a preborn life. Only 40 to 50 percent of fetuses survive to become persons in the full sense. A fetus belongs to the mother until it attains personhood and is morally subject to any action she wishes to take with it.

Second, abortion must be protected as an alternative for women who are the victims of rape or incest. While this number is admittedly small in this country (approximately 1 percent of all abortions), it is growing in many countries around the world. As many as one in three women may become the victim of such an attack. They must be spared the further trauma of pregnancy and childbirth, it is claimed.

Third, no unwanted children should be brought into the world. If a woman does not wish to bear a child, she clearly will not be an appropriate or effective mother if the child is born. Given the population explosion occurring in many countries of the world, abortion is a necessary option for women who do not want children. The woman is more closely involved with the fetus than any other individual and is the best person to determine whether or not this child is wanted and will receive proper care.

Fourth, the state has no right to legislate our personal moral decisions. The government has no authority to restrict homosexuality, consensual sex, cigarette consumption, or other individual decisions which many people consider to be wrong. Since there is no constitutional standard for when life begins, decisions made regarding a fetus are likewise a matter of individual morality.

The state should impose legislation on moral questions only when this legislation expresses the clear moral consensus of the community and when it prevents conduct that obviously threatens the public welfare. Nearly everyone condemns murder, for instance, and believes that it threatens us all. But Americans are divided on the morality of abortion. It is hard to see how aborting a fetus threatens the rest of the community.

And so, it is claimed, abortion should not be subject to governmental control. It is better to allow a mother to make this decision than to legislate it through governmental action. Many who personally consider abortion to be wrong are persuaded by this argument and thus support the "pro-choice" rather than "pro-abortion" position.

Fifth, the rights and concerns of the mother must take precedence over those of the fetus. Even if we grant fetuses limited rights, they must not supersede the rights of mothers since the latter are clearly persons under the Constitution. If we allow abortion to protect her physical life, we should do so to protect her emotional health or quality of life as well.

This was one of the Court's most significant arguments, as it sought to protect the mother's mental and physical health. Many "pro-choice" advocates are especially persuaded by this argument and view the abortion debate within the context of a woman's right to control her own life.

Moral arguments against abortion

"Pro-life" advocates counter each of these claims with their own ethical arguments.

First, they assert that a fetus is a human life and should be granted the full protection of the law. The fetus carries its parents' genetic code and is a distinct person. It does not yet possess self-consciousness, reasoning ability, or moral awareness (the usual descriptions of a "person"), but neither do newborns or young children. As this is the central issue of the debate, we'll say more about it in a moment.

Second, most "pro-life" advocates are willing to permit abortion in cases of rape or incest or to protect the life of the mother. Since such cases typically account for only 1 percent of abortions performed, limiting abortion to these conditions would prevent the vast majority of abortions occurring in America.

Third, "pro-life" advocates agree that all children should be wanted, so they argue strongly for adoption as an alternative to abortion. They also assert that an unwanted child would rather live than die. By "pro-choice" logic, it would be possible to argue for infanticide and all forms of euthanasia as well as abortion.

Fourth, "pro-life" supporters do not see abortion legislation as an intrusion into areas of private morality. Protecting the rights of the individual is the state's first responsibility. No moral state can overlook murder, whatever the personal opinions of those who commit it. The state is especially obligated to protect the rights of those who cannot defend themselves.

But what of the claim that legislation must always reflect the clear will of the majority and protect the public welfare? The collective will of the culture must never supersede what is right and wrong. For instance, heroin is so popular that as many as 4.2 million Americans say they've used it at least once. Nonetheless, we ban it because its harmful effects are clear to medical science. The effects of abortion on a fetus are obviously even more disastrous to the fetus. And just because society is unclear as to when life begins does not mean that the question is unknowable.

If more of the public understood the physical and ethical issues involved in abortion, the large majority would consider abortion to be a threat to public welfare. Abortion threatens the entire community in three ways:

1. Abortion ends the lives of millions, on a level exceeding all wars and disasters combined.

2. Abortion encourages sexual promiscuity.

3. Abortion permits women to make a choice that will plague many of them with guilt for years to come.

And so, abortion meets the standard for legislative relevance and must be addressed and limited or abolished by the state.

Fifth, "pro-life" advocates want to encourage the health of both the mother and the child and do not believe that we must choose between the two. As the rights of a mother are no more important than those of her newborn infant, so they are no more important than those of her preborn child. The stress, guilt, and long-term mental anguish reported by many who abort their children must be considered. The legal right to abortion subjects a woman to pressure from her husband or sexual partner to end her pregnancy. Killing the fetus for the sake of the mother's health is like remedying paranoia by killing all the imagined persecutors. For these reasons, "pro-life" advocates argue that a moral state must limit or prevent abortion.

When does life begin?

This is obviously the crucial question in the abortion debate. If life does not begin until the fetus is viable or the child is born, one can argue that the "right to life" does not extend to the preborn and abortion should be considered both legal and moral. But if life begins at conception, there can be no moral justification for abortion since this action kills an innocent person.

There are essentially three answers to our question.

1. *Functionalism* states that the fetus is a "person" when it can act personally as a moral, intellectual, and spiritual agent. (Note that by this definition, some question whether a newborn infant would be considered a "person.")

2. *Actualism* is the position that a fetus is a person if it possesses the potential for developing self-conscious, personal life. This definition would permit abortion when the fetus clearly does not possess the capacity for functional life.

3. *Essentialism* argues that the fetus is a person from conception, whatever its health or potential. It is an individual in the earliest stages of development and deserves all the protections afforded to other persons by our society.

Our Declaration of Independence begins, "We hold these truths to be self-evident: that all men are created equal; that they are endowed by their creator with certain unalienable rights; that among these are life, liberty, and the pursuit of happiness." If an unborn child is considered a person, it possesses the "unalienable" right to life as well.

So, can we determine when life begins? Our answer depends on the definition of "life." A "pro-choice" advocate recognizes that the fetus is alive in the sense that it is a biological entity. But so is every other part of a woman's body. Some consider the fetus to be a "growth" and liken it to a tumor or other unwanted tissue. Biology alone is not enough to settle the issue.

What about capacity? Many ethicists define a "person" as someone able to respond to stimuli, interact with others, and make individual decisions. A fetus meets the first two standards from almost the moment of its conception and clearly cannot fulfill the third only because it is enclosed in its mother's body. Would a newborn baby fulfill these three conditions?

What about individuality? If we view a fetus as a "growth" within the mother's body, it would be easier to sanction her choice to remove that growth if she wishes. But a fetus is distinct from its mother from the moment of its conception. It is alive—it reacts to stimuli and can produce its own cells and develop them into a specific pattern of maturity. It is human, completely distinguishable from all other living organisms, possessing all forty-six human chromosomes, and able to develop only into a human being. And it is complete—nothing new will be added except the growth and development of what exists from the moment of conception.

It is a scientific fact that every abortion performed in the United States is performed on a being so fully formed that its heart is beating and its brain activity can be measured on an EEG machine. At twelve weeks, the unborn baby is only about two inches long, yet every organ of the human body is clearly in place.

Theologian Karl Barth described the fetus well:

> The embryo has its own autonomy, its own brain, its own nervous system, its own blood circulation. If its life is affected by that of the mother, it also affects hers. It can have its own illnesses in which the mother has no part. Conversely, it may be quite healthy even though the mother is seriously ill. It may die while the mother continues to live. It may also continue to live after its mother's death and be eventually saved by a timely operation on her dead body. In short, it is a human being in its own right.

And note that you did not come from a fetus—you *were* a fetus. A "fetus" is simply a human life in the womb. It becomes a "baby" outside the womb. But it is the same physical entity in either place.

For these reasons, "pro-life" advocates believe that the US Supreme Court was wrong in deciding that a fetus is not a person entitled to the full protections of the law. Apart from spiritual or moral concerns, it is a simple fact of biology that the fetus possesses every attribute of human life we find in a newborn infant, with the exception of independent physical viability. Left unharmed, it will soon develop this capacity as well. If a life must be independently viable to be viewed as a person, a young child might well fail this standard, as would those of any age facing severe physical challenges.

What about rape and incest?

The Bible makes rape a capital offense: "If in the open country a man meets a young woman who is betrothed, and the man seizes her and lies with her, then only the man who lay with her shall die. But you shall do nothing to the young woman; she has committed no offense punishable by death. For this case is like that of a man attacking and murdering his neighbor" (Deuteronomy 22:25–26).

God's word clearly condemns such a crime against women. "Pro-choice" advocates often point to this issue early in the debate, arguing that a woman should not continue to be victimized by bearing a child as the result of such a horrific crime.

Unprotected intercourse results in pregnancy about 4 percent of the time. If one in three women is likely to be raped in her lifetime, and incestuous relationships subject a woman to repeated sexual abuse, pregnancies resulting from rape and incest are so likely that abortion must be legal as a remedy for women subjected to such crime. Nearly all pro-life advocates concede the point, allowing for abortion in the case of rape or incest.

However, since rape and incest victims represent approximately 1 percent of the abortion cases recorded annually in this country, a decision to limit abortions to this exception would prevent the deaths of nearly all of the babies who are aborted each year. Only about 3 percent of the abortions performed each year in America relate to the health of the mother, and 3 percent relate to the health of the child. Ninety-three percent are elective.

To allow for abortion because of the very rare incidence of abortions performed due to rape and incest is something like suspending all heroin laws because of the small number of patients who could benefit from its medicinal effects. We could stop the use of traffic lights because of the incidents when they slow a sick person's rush to a hospital, but would we not cause more harm than we prevent?

At the same time, Americans must be conscious of the fact that rape and incest are far more common in some other countries and cultures. Rape in particular is a typical means of coercion and military control in some societies. There the percentage of abortions related to rape may be much higher than is the case in America.

This caveat stated, I'm not sure that even this decision is the moral choice. I must quickly admit that my status as an American white male makes it impossible for me to identify with women who have experienced rape and incest. But it is hard for me to understand how the child which is produced by this terrible crime does not deserve to live.

Ethel Waters, the famous gospel singer, was the product of a rape. So was a student I taught at Southwestern Seminary, an evangelist with a global ministry today. I tread very lightly here but would at the very least suggest that this issue is far from the primary cause of abortion in America today.

It is vital that we be pro-life, not just pro-birth. We should care for the mother, father, and family as well as the unborn child. Many women who choose abortion do so for financial reasons—we should seek resources to help them bear this burden so they can choose to give their children life.

In addition, we should advocate for adoption as well as against abortion.

And we should respond to this issue by "speaking the truth in love" (Ephesians 4:15). Abortion is a tragedy that affects the biological parents and extended family as well as the unborn child. We are called to offer grace and truth to all.

The Bible and prostitution

A movement to legalize prostitution is growing in the US. At this writing, Oregon's House Judiciary Committee is considering a bill that would decriminalize so-called "sex work." The ACLU has come out in support of this movement with an article titled, "Sex Work is Real Work, and it's Time to Treat it That Way." When Vice President Kamala Harris was running for president in 2019, she voiced her support as well.

Advocates claim that "criminalization of sex work contributes to community violence, propagates crime, blocks access to public health resources, is an ineffective deterrent to participation in sex work, and is deeply harmful to sex workers." They add that criminalizing sex work causes workers to fear the police, making them less likely to ask for help if they face danger from a client. They say it also makes it harder for sex workers to access health care, welfare benefits, and social services.

However, supporters of decriminalizing "sex work" should acknowledge the risks for "sex workers."

A self-described feminist writes that "prostitution is inherently abusive, and a cause and a consequence of women's inequality." One study of prostituted women in nine countries found that 70 to 95 percent were physically assaulted; 60 to 75 percent were raped; and 89 percent told researchers that they urgently wanted to escape prostitution.

In addition, the US Department of State warns that "where prostitution is legalized or tolerated, there is a greater demand for human trafficking victims and nearly always an increase in the number of women and children trafficked into commercial sex slavery." A study published by Harvard Law School reported that "countries with legalized prostitution are associated with higher human trafficking inflows than countries where prostitution is prohibited."

Once again, adopting biblical morality would prevent such suffering by millions of victims of prostitution around the globe.

The Bible and pornography

Every day in America, 37 pornographic videos are created, 2.5 billion emails containing porn are sent and received, 68 million internet searches are generated related to pornography (25 percent of total searches), and 116,000 queries are received related to child pornography. Forty million Americans regularly visit porn sites (one-third are women).

It is often claimed that porn is entertainment and should be protected as free speech. How harmful is pornography?

Effects on men

Studies have found that viewing people's bodies, as opposed to their faces, makes us judge those people as less intelligent, less ambitious, less competent, and less likable. One neuroimaging experiment found that when men viewed pictures of sexualized women, this action lowered activity in brain regions associated with thinking about other people's minds.

Effects on women

Pornography degrades and brutalizes women. It utilizes three basic themes:

1. All women want sex from all men at all times.

2. Women enjoy every sex act that men perform or demand.

3. Any woman who does not realize this at first can be "turned on" easily with a little force.

Many women involved in pornographic photos and videos are being exploited by force and coercion. Psychological and physical damage is common, as is heavy alcohol and drug use. In addition, pornography leads men to degrade and dehumanize women. According to one expert: "As pornography has become more acceptable, both legally and culturally, the level of brutality toward, and degradation of, women has intensified."

Gail Dines, author of *Pornland: How Porn Has Hijacked Our Sexuality*, warns: "We are now bringing up a generation of boys on cruel, violent porn. . . . Given what we know about how images affect people, this is going to have a profound influence on their sexuality, behavior and attitudes toward women."

Effects on children and youth

Another expert notes: "There is evidence that the prevalence of pornography in the lives of many children and adolescents is far more significant than most adults realize, that pornography is deforming the healthy sexual development of these young viewers, and that it is used to exploit children and adolescents."

A study of 804 representative Italian teenagers found that boys who viewed pornography were significantly more likely to report having "sexually harassed a peer or having forced somebody to have sex." Men who habitually view pornography have a higher tolerance for abnormal sexual behaviors, sexual aggression, promiscuity, and rape. Some begin to view women and even children as "sex objects."

There is abundant evidence that pornography is being used by adolescents to coerce one another into sexual behavior. In one study, twenty-nine of thirty juvenile sex offenders had been exposed to X-rated magazines or videos. Amid rising evidence that watching porn leads to sexual assault, India banned more than eight hundred pornographic websites (only to partially lift the ban after receiving criticism).

In addition to the effects of porn on youth, we should consider ways adolescents are victimized by the porn industry. An estimated 293,000 American youths are currently at risk of becoming victims of commercial sexual exploitation. The majority of these victims are runaway or "throwaway" youths who live on the streets and become involved with prostitution.

In a study of arrested child pornography possessors, 40 percent were found to have sexually victimized children. Child pornography has now become a $20 billion industry annually. Approximately thirty million children have been sexually exploited in the last thirty years; the average age of a trafficked victim is twelve to fourteen years old.

Adults who chronically consume pornography become visually desensitized and eventually begin viewing depictions they would have previously rejected as off-limits. For instance, numerous users report to clinicians the slippery slope from viewing pornography featuring adults to viewing child pornography. Such desensitization can lead to other forms of violence as well.

Effects on marriage

According to the American Academy of Matrimonial Lawyers:

- 68 percent of divorce cases involve one party meeting a new paramour over the internet.

- 56 percent involve one party having an obsessive interest in pornographic websites.

- 47 percent involve spending excessive time on a computer.

- 33 percent involve spending excessive time in chat rooms.

Get help now

If you or someone you know is struggling with pornography, get help now. Scripture teaches that we are responsible to help and encourage one another: "Brothers, if anyone is caught in any transgression, you who are spiritual should restore him in a spirit of gentleness. Keep watch on yourself, lest you too be tempted. Bear one another's burdens, and so fulfill the law of Christ" (Galatians 6:1–2).

Christian counseling is a very important way God uses his people to minister to one another. Most of us carry baggage after years of living in a fallen world. A wise counselor can help us discover areas of unforgiveness, shame, and guilt, some of which may motivate involvement in pornography.

There is no shame in seeking out such help. Proverbs 20:5 says, "The purpose in a man's heart is like deep water, but a man of understanding will draw it out." Most Christian leaders have mentors and counselors whom they trust regularly for wisdom and advice. Your church leaders can recommend excellent resources in your area.

Support groups for those battling addiction are another tool used by the Spirit to heal God's people. One excellent option is Celebrate Recovery (CR), a Christ-centered program using a form of the twelve-step program pioneered by Alcoholics Anonymous. CR groups generally meet weekly and have helped thousands of believers recover from addictions. As with Christian counseling, these groups are confidential. To see if a group meets in your area, consult their website at celebraterecovery.com.

For pastors struggling with pornography, confidential online communities and resources are becoming more common. Covenant Eyes has a page with resources for pastors who battle this issue at covenanteyes.com/resources-for-pastors. And I highly recommend There's Still Hope, a ministry led by my brother and his wife for pastors and others who are struggling with sexual addiction.

Remember God's promise: "We are more than conquerors through him who loved us" (Romans 8:37).

Pornography, like all sin, will always take us further than we wanted to go, keep us longer than we wanted to stay, and cost us more than we wanted to pay. But "he who is in you is greater than he who is in the world" (1 John 4:4).

Redeeming the attack on biblical morality

Evangelicals can join God in redeeming the cultural conflict over sexual morality if we will make two commitments: speak the truth in love and offer hope in Christ.

Speak the truth in love

It is a tragic fact that evangelicals have not always responded to the LGBTQ community in ways that honor Jesus and demonstrate his compassion for all people. The opposite has sometimes been true, in fact.

Matthew Lee Anderson serves as an assistant research professor of ethics and theology at Baylor University. Writing as an evangelical theologian, his expansive article in *Christianity Today* titled "How We Got to the Equality Act" should be required reading for all evangelicals in America.

The subtitle of his article captures his argument: "The LGBT movement was shaped by the animosity of populist evangelical rhetoric and tactics." Anderson takes us back to 1977, when Anita Bryant campaigned against Miami's recently passed nondiscrimination ordinance. Bryant, a former beauty contest winner and a Top 40 singer, was at the time the face of the Florida Citrus Commission.

Her efforts included rhetoric about the threat that gay people ostensibly posed to children and became the campaign's lasting legacy. She won her campaign in Miami, then established Save Our Children, an organization intended to restrict LGBT rights, and promised to do for the nation what she had done for Miami.

Billy Graham was asked about her. While praising her courage and lauding her for "emphasizing that God loves the homosexual," Dr. Graham also stated that he would not have said "some things she and her associates said . . . in the same way."

Anderson then reviews a series of legislative attempts by evangelicals. One would have required schools to fire LGBT teachers; others worked to prevent nondiscrimination ordinances. The television campaign intentionally presented gay pride parades in the most flamboyant manner possible. One evangelical activist even compared gay people to maggots.

Anderson notes:

> For evangelicals to speak uncompromisingly about the goods of marriage and the integrity of the body, we must face up to our failures to do so in the past. The LGBT community has its own missteps and mistakes to account for. But as any good evangelical knows, denouncing the sins of others does not exonerate one's own. . . .
>
> By honestly recounting our missteps, evangelicals might give progressive LGBT activists a reason to look afresh at our convictions about marriage and the body. We exhibit confidence, not accommodation of weakness, when we forthrightly acknowledge our failures to embody the truths we affirm.

We have noted that all humans are broken sexually. We are all equally in need of grace. When we share God's word from a heart of humility that seeks to pay forward the transforming love we have experienced, we align our spirits with the Holy Spirit. When we act with judgmental condemnation, we undermine our witness and grieve our Lord.

Offer hope in Christ

Christians in Corinth were living in one of the most immoral places in the world. As a busy seaport and trade center, the city saw sailors and merchants from around the world, many of whom brought horrific decadence to her streets. The Acrocorinth, a hill rising 1,886 feet above the city, was the location of a temple to Diana (Aphrodite); ancient historians claimed that as many as a thousand temple prostitutes worked there.

Consequently, to *corinthianize* was to commit immorality. The city was Sodom and Gomorrah, Las Vegas, and Bourbon Street in one.

As a result, Paul had to warn the Corinthians, "Do not be deceived: neither the sexually immoral, nor idolaters, nor adulterers, nor men who practice homosexuality, nor thieves, nor the greedy, nor drunkards, nor revilers, nor swindlers will inherit the kingdom of God" (1 Corinthians 6:9–10). Unsurprisingly, he added, "And such were some of you" (v. 11a).

Then came the words that capture the hope of the gospel: "But you were washed, you were sanctified, you were justified in the name of the Lord Jesus Christ and by the Spirit of our God" (v. 11b).

Jesus can change any person who is willing to be changed.

Across the decades of my ministry, I have met men and women who have been delivered from same-sex attraction and behavior. I have also met men and women who have been delivered from addiction to pornography, couples who were devastated by adultery but whose marriages have been made new, and single adults who have been liberated from the immorality of their culture to live with biblical purity.

Nowhere is the hope of the gospel more urgently needed than here. Nowhere does our culture need evangelicals to proclaim biblical truth more courageously and compassionately.

When we invite those we know to trust Christ with their sexual brokenness, we are offering them the path to healing and peace, redemption and transformation.

We are beggars helping beggars find bread, to the glory of God.

"I have a dream that my four little children will one day live in a nation where they are not judged by the color of their skin but by the content of their character."—**DR. MARTIN LUTHER KING JR**

11

Defending biblical equality with compassion and humility

Senator Dick Durbin (D-IL.) is a practicing Catholic Christian. His denomination has consistently stated its opposition to the Equality Act on the grounds that it discriminates against Christians and threatens the unborn.

Nonetheless, when the Senate Judiciary Committee held a hearing on the Act in March 2021, the senator stated: "I do believe that people who want to blatantly discriminate and use religion as their weapon have gone too far. We have to have limits on what they can do. I might remind us in history that the Ku Klux Klan was not burning question marks. They were burning a cross. They were making some distorted connection with religion. And God forbid that anyone would buy that. We don't need that in America, regardless of the time, regardless of the organization, wherever they come down on the political spectrum."

If Catholics and others who support biblical morality are to be equated with KKK members, clearly evangelicals are facing a cultural tsunami.

As we observed in chapter 3, Critical Theory and other ideologies are being used to claim that Christians, especially white evangelicals, are racists who oppress minorities. While this is a very expansive subject, we can survey some responses that will equip us to defend ourselves and our faith from these charges.

Racism in history

It is tragic that racism, defined as discrimination against a person or group based on their race or ethnicity, is a fact of human history.

Moses' brother and sister "spoke against Moses because of the Cushite woman whom he had married" (Numbers 12:1). Cush was a region south of Ethiopia; its people were known for their black skin (Jeremiah 13:23). When Moses' brother and sister spoke against him for marrying his Cushite wife, God rebuked them (Numbers 12:4–15).

Thomas Sowell, a brilliant economist and social theorist at Stanford University's Hoover Institution, noted that "from 1500 to 1800, more than a million Europeans were enslaved by North African pirates." He added that slavery was common in Europe, Asia, Polynesia, China, and parts of Southeast Asia, where slaves were a majority of the population. He also reported that slavery was established in the Western Hemisphere before Columbus and that the Ottoman Empire regularly enslaved a percentage of young boys from the Balkans, converting them to Islam and assigning them to various duties.

Tragically, in what became America, many European explorers characterized the indigenous peoples they encountered as "heathen" and considered their race and culture to be inferior. Many who supported the enslavement of Africans likewise viewed them as inferior to white people. Such claims were used to justify the system of chattel slavery (the personal ownership of another person) that enslaved millions of Africans. Many slaveholders convinced themselves that African slaves, due to their supposedly inferior nature, were better off and better cared for in European bondage than in African freedom.

This racist ideology led directly to America's "original sin," the institution of slavery in the New World. The first group of African slaves arrived at Jamestown, Virginia, in 1619. Planters quickly realized that enormous profits could be gained from importing enslaved laborers.

Africans could be made to work much longer and harder in the fields. Since they were so far from Africa, they could not easily escape and return home. In addition, African slaves came from a variety of nations and cultures and thus could not easily communicate with one another to organize resistance. Most slaves came from West Africa, where some tribal leaders were willing to capture and sell other Africans for profit. Slaves became especially important to the economy of the South, where the climate and topography were more suitable for tobacco and cotton plantations.

While the Declaration of Independence claimed that "all men are created equal," the US Constitution determined that enslaved persons would be counted as "three-fifths of all other Persons" for purposes of government representation and taxation (Article I, Section II, Paragraph III). The Constitution permitted importing slaves until 1808, with a tax of $10 per slave (Article I, Section IX, Clause I). And it required those living in free states to return escaped slaves to their owners (Article IV, Section II, Clause III).

Slavery was legal in America until 1865 and the adoption of the Thirteenth Amendment. The Fourteenth Amendment (1868) guaranteed the same rights to all male citizens; the Fifteenth Amendment (1870) made it illegal to deprive any eligible citizen of the right to vote, regardless of color.

However, segregation was legal until the Supreme Court struck it down in 1954 in *Brown v. Board of Education*. Jim Crow laws enforcing racial segregation were overturned by the Civil Rights Act of 1964 and the Voting Rights Act of 1965.

What the Bible says about racism

One: We are all created by God.

The human story begins in Genesis 1, where God "created man in his own image, in the image of God he created him; male and female he created them" (v. 27). Every person is created intentionally by God in his own divine image. Thus, every person is sacred and equally valuable. Every form of racism, by definition, is to be rejected.

Two: We are all descended from the same parents.

Every human being is descended from Adam and Eve (Genesis 1:28). As a result, "The man called his wife's name Eve, because she was the mother of all living" (Genesis 3:20). As Scripture notes, the Lord "made from one man every nation of mankind to live on all the face of the earth" (Acts 17:26). Because of the Flood, all of humanity can trace our ancestry to Noah as well (Genesis 9:1).

Three: Every person is equally valuable to God.

As noted earlier, Paul stated boldly: "There is neither Jew nor Greek, there is neither slave nor free, there is no male and female, for you are all one in Christ Jesus" (Galatians 3:28). This was written at a time when many Jews considered Greeks to be unclean and inferior. Some claimed that God made Gentiles so there would be "firewood in hell." Many refused even to look upon a Gentile in public.

For their part, Gentiles persecuted the Jewish people across nearly their entire history. The Jews were enslaved by Egypt, attacked by Canaanites and other surrounding tribes, destroyed by Assyria, enslaved by Babylon, and ruled by Persia, Greece, and Rome. The Roman Empire destroyed their temple in AD 70 and disbanded their nation after the Bar Kokhba revolt in AD 132–135. Nonetheless, Scripture teaches that "there is neither Jew nor Greek" in the eyes of God.

"There is neither slave nor free" was also a revolutionary claim. As we have seen, slavery was endemic in the first-century world. Many viewed slaves, especially those who came from foreign lands, as inferior to Romans.

"There is no male and female" was a radical statement as well. Romans considered women to be the possessions of men. A female belonged to her father until she belonged to her husband. Women were either wives or concubines with few rights of their own.

Galatians 3:28 sounds the clarion call that every form of racism known to Paul's day was invalid and sinful. The God who made us all loves us all. Paul repeated his assertion to the Colossians: "There is not Greek and Jew, circumcised and uncircumcised, barbarian, Scythian, slave, free; but Christ is all, and in all" (Colossians 3:11).

To summarize: "God shows no partiality" (Acts 10:34).

Four: Each person is equally welcome to salvation in Christ.

God loves all sinners and wants all to come to faith in his Son: "God shows his love for us in that while we were still sinners, Christ died for us" (Romans 5:8). Our Lord "is patient toward you, not wishing that any should perish, but that all should reach repentance" (2

Peter 3:9). As Paul noted, God "desires all people to be saved and to come to the knowledge of the truth" (1 Timothy 2:4). That's why the apostle could testify: "I am not ashamed of the gospel, for it is the power of God for salvation to everyone who believes, to the Jew first and also to the Greek" (Romans 1:16).

Our Father's saving love is available to all: "There is no distinction between Jew and Greek; for the same Lord is Lord of all, bestowing his riches on all who call on him" (Romans 10:12). His grace is universal: "For God so loved the world, that he gave his only Son, that whoever believes in him should not perish but have eternal life" (John 3:16).

When we trust in Christ, we become one people: "He himself is our peace, who has made us both one and has broken down in his flesh the dividing wall of hostility" (Ephesians 2:14). As a result, "In one Spirit we were all baptized into one body—Jews or Greeks, slaves or free—and all were made to drink of one Spirit" (1 Corinthians 12:13).

Jesus "is the propitiation for our sins, and not for ours only but also for the sins of the whole world" (1 John 2:2). Peter told his fellow Jewish Christians that God "made no distinction between us and [Gentile Christians], having cleansed their hearts by faith" (Acts 15:9). As a result, we are to "make disciples of all nations" (Matthew 28:19). "Nations" translates *ethnos*, meaning people groups. We get "ethnicity" from this word. Every person of every ethnicity is to be brought to Christ through the ministry of the church.

Five: All people will be equally valuable in paradise.

John was given this vision of heaven: "After this I looked, and behold, a great multitude that no one could number, from every nation, from all tribes and peoples and languages, standing before the throne and before the Lamb, clothed in white robes, with palm branches in their hands" (Revelation 7:9).

Six: We are to love all people unconditionally.

God's word is blunt: "If you show partiality, you are committing sin and are convicted by the law as transgressors" (James 2:9). "Partiality" translates *prosopolempsia*, meaning to show favoritism or prejudice, to treat one person as inherently better than another. Such prejudice is sin.

The Lord told his people: "You shall treat the stranger who sojourns with you as the native among you, and you shall love him as yourself, for you were strangers in the land of Egypt" (Leviticus 19:34). Jesus taught us: "Whatever you wish that others would do to you, do also to them, for this is the Law and the Prophets" (Matthew 7:12). We are to "love your neighbor as yourself" (Matthew 22:39, quoting Leviticus 19:18).

Peter testified to the Gentiles who sought to hear the gospel: "You yourselves know how unlawful it is for a Jew to associate with or to visit anyone of another nation, but God has shown me that I should not call any person common or unclean" (Acts 10:28).

Three common questions

In defending the Bible against the charge of racism, we may encounter the following questions.

One: What about the "mark of Cain"?

After Cain murdered his brother, God sentenced him to be "a fugitive and a wanderer on the earth" (Genesis 4:12). Cain protested that "I shall be a fugitive and a wanderer on the earth, and whoever finds me will kill me" (v. 14). God replied, "Not so! If anyone kills Cain, vengeance shall be taken on him sevenfold" (v. 15a). Then, "the LORD put a mark on Cain, lest any who found him should attack him" (v. 15b).

The Hebrew word translated "mark" is *ot*, referring to a sign or token. It is used eighty times in the Old Testament; not once does it refer to skin color. Nonetheless, some have identified this "mark" with being black. Since Cain was cursed for his sin against his brother, it was claimed that those whose skin was black were his descendants and were cursed by God. This claim was used to justify the enslavement of Africans.

This line of reasoning is completely wrong. As noted, the "mark" of Cain had nothing to do with his skin color. In addition, Cain's family line probably died in the Flood. Clearly, the "mark of Cain" has nothing to do with being Black.

Two: What about the "curse of Ham"?

Ham was one of Noah's three sons. Ham had four sons: Cush, Egypt, Put, and Canaan (Genesis 10:6). Ham is considered the father of Black people since some of his descendants settled in Africa. According to tradition, Cush settled in Ethiopia, south of Egypt; Egypt (also known as "Mizraim") settled in the land of Egypt; Put settled in Libya; Canaan settled above Africa and east of the Mediterranean Sea.

The Bible tells us that after the Flood, Noah became drunk (Genesis 9:21). Then "Ham, the father of Canaan, saw the nakedness of his father and told his two brothers outside" (v. 22). Shem and Japheth "covered the nakedness of their father" (v. 23). After Noah awoke, he said, "Cursed be Canaan; a servant of servants shall he be to his brothers" (v. 25).

Note that Noah cursed Canaan, not Ham. Thus, his curse was irrelevant to Ham's sons who had settled in Africa and their descendants. Also note that Noah's curse was specifically directed at Canaan, with no mention of his descendants. If Noah's curse was applied to his descendants, it related to the Canaanites living in the land that became Israel. It had nothing whatsoever to do with Black people.

Nonetheless, the Old Scofield Reference Bible of 1909 (often considered the authoritative Bible of fundamentalist Christians) interprets Genesis 9:24–25 to teach: "A prophetic declaration is made that from Ham will descend an inferior and servile posterity."

With his typically brilliant exposition, Dr. Tony Evans addresses this issue, noting that biblical curses are limited to three or four generations (Exodus 20:5) and are reversed when people repent and return to obedience (Exodus 20:6). As Dr. Evans shows, Scripture consistently rebukes and rejects the claim that Black people (or any other race) are inferior to any other.

Three: Didn't slavery proponents use the Bible to justify their position?

Tragically, many who supported slavery in the antebellum South used the "mark of Cain" and "curse of Ham" to justify their position. They also noted biblical statements encouraging slaves to obey their masters.

As we saw earlier, the Bible deals realistically with the practice where necessary, but it clearly endorses the intrinsically sacred value of each person. The biblical emphasis on the sanctity of life was one of the key motivating factors for William Wilberforce and others who worked so sacrificially to abolish slavery.

Like any other book, the Bible can be misused by those who misinterpret and misrepresent its teachings. For instance, when chloroform was developed, some were resistant to using it for women in childbirth since Genesis 3:16 teaches "in pain you shall bring forth children."

When oil wells were first dug in Pennsylvania, many New York ministers opposed the project on the grounds that it would deplete the oil stored for the predestined burning of the world (2 Peter 3:10, 12). And winnowing fans were rejected by Christians who thought they interfered with the providence of God since "the wind blows where it wishes" (John 3:8).

When a doctor misuses medicine, we blame the physician, not the science. When an attorney misrepresents a legal statute, we blame the lawyer, not the law. In responding to racists who misused the Bible to justify slavery, we should blame the racists, not the word of God.

Redeeming the attack on biblical equality

As we have seen, the charge that evangelicals are oppressors can be countered logically and biblically. But our most effective response is often more personal than propositional. When our opponents see the inclusive grace of God at work in and through our lives, they will be drawn to such grace for themselves. To this end, let's use this issue to renew our commitment to inclusivity and compassion. I suggest three steps.

One: Search your own heart.

Ask the Holy Spirit to show you any attitudes, emotions, words, or actions which are racist, then confess all that comes to your thoughts. If you have harmed another person through such sin, seek to make restitution (Matthew 5:23–24).

Two: Ask for accountability.

We can be guilty of racism without realizing it. I encourage you to speak with a friend of a different race, especially one who is Black. Ask them to show you anything you have said or done that they perceive to be racist, even if this was not your intent. Then take steps to confess and seek reconciliation where needed.

Three: Build relational bridges.

How can you use your influence to build relationships across racial divides? How can you work for the common good with those of a different race or ethnicity? Where could you, your family, your church, or your organization make a difference for the cause of unity in grace?

How can you demonstrate the inclusive love of Jesus in your life and witness?

St. Augustine noted that God loves each of us as if there were only one of us.

Now it's our turn.

"Culture is the root of politics, and religion is the root of culture."
—**RICHARD JOHN NEUHAUS**

12

Defending biblical Christians with courage and hope

Poison hemlock has been called one of the "deadliest plants in North America." Eating it can cause respiratory failure and death. Even touching it can cause blisters. Its relative, the spotted water hemlock, is even worse: eating it causes death within two hours. It grows across North America. Looking at pictures of both plants online, I would never imagine that they are so dangerous. They produce small but attractive flowers and seem harmless. But botanists warn us that looks can be deceiving and, in this case, deadly.

We are hearing similar warnings with regard to evangelicals in America. As we noted in chapter 4, advocates of a rising secular religion see us as an obstacle, perhaps the primary obstacle, in their path. Evangelical Christianity has gone from being central to culture to peripheral and is now viewed as dangerous to society.

Harold O. J. Brown notes that the US has "transform[ed] the principle of non-establishment (of a state church) to a radical separation of church and state, which by the end of the twentieth century has increasingly come to mean the radical exclusion of all that is religious, and particularly of all that is Christian, from visibility in public life." He adds: "This gradual abandonment of the Christian heritage of Western nations has now become a deliberate rejection."

Let's respond to this rejection with logic, evidence, and the witness of personal transformation.

Is religion dangerous?

Consider four reasoned responses.

One: "Dangerous" must be defined.

Terrorism such as 9/11 is clearly dangerous on a horrific level to those who are its victims. But the issue is more complicated than it may seem.

I once spoke at a meeting of the Men of Nehemiah in Dallas, Texas. Their ministry works with previously incarcerated men, teaching them job skills and helping them deal with substance abuse issues. They are located in a crime-ridden part of Dallas. Some would say it was dangerous for me to park my car there and walk into their building. Many who join this organization leave gangs, exposing themselves or their families to retribution. On the other hand, those who join the Men of Nehemiah are significantly less likely to return to prison or to criminal behavior.

How are we to judge the danger inherent in their ministry?

As we noted in chapter 9, those who attacked America on 9/11 would not have called themselves "terrorists," but "martyrs." In their view, the West has been attacking the Muslim world since the Crusades. They saw our military intervention in Iraq and Afghanistan not as self-defense but as an extension of Western imperialism. Since they consider America to be a Christian nation, they would cite our military actions as examples of a "dangerous" religion.

Of course, I would not suggest that these assertions are correct. On the contrary, most of the Muslim world views them as a horrific contradiction of Islam. My point is that "danger" must be defined. What seems dangerous to some is considered righteous to others. This is a simple fact of logic, one that answers the easy criticism by atheists that "all religion is dangerous" or "religion poisons everything."

Two: There is no such thing as "religion."

In 2009 I was privileged to participate in a debate with Christopher Hitchens. I assumed that his bestseller *god is not Great: How Religion Poisons Everything* would be central to the discussion. In reading it, I was astonished to see how often he considers all religions as one and condemns all for the perceived crimes of some.

In point of fact, there is no such thing as "religion" per se. What color is it? How much does it weigh? There are only religions—specific manifestations of religious principles and commitments. Just as there is no such thing as "leaves," only individual leafs, so it is with "religion."

When critics claim that "religion poisons everything," we need to ask if this is true of each and every religion. Has the skeptic investigated every one? *The World Christian Encyclopedia* states that there are more than ten thousand distinct religions in the world. Has the critic studied Bulgyohwoi (a distinct variant of Buddhism), for instance?

It would be different if the world's religions believed and taught essentially the same beliefs, but they do not. If Islam is correct about the afterlife, Buddhism is wrong. If Hinduism is right about the existence of thousands (some say millions) of gods, Judaism is wrong. These are not different roads up the same mountain, but very different mountains.

Imagine condemning all "medicine" because of the crimes of some doctors, or all "art" because of the excesses of some artists. The illogic of Dawkins' claim that "religion is the root of all evil" is clear. In fact, it is the kind of non-fact-based rhetorical statement he so often accuses religious people of making.

Three: Evil acts are clearly not confined to religion.

The twentieth century was the most bloody, war-torn era in human history. And yet each of its major wars was fought for political reasons, none of them religious in motivation. Are we to determine that "all politics are dangerous" and seek to restrict or abolish their activities?

Nuclear science has given us sustainable energy as well as atomic weapons and crises such as Chernobyl and Fukushima. Are we to castigate all nuclear scientists as dangerous?

Democracy is clearly one of the greatest forces for liberation and progress in human history. And yet it perpetuated slavery in America, an institution that was abolished only after the bloodiest war in our nation's history. It has perpetuated abortion, leading to the deaths of more than sixty-two million babies. In the minds of some critics of religion, it permitted an "unjust" war in Iraq. Are we to abolish democracy and vilify its participants?

Four: Religion is not to blame for its misuse.

The same hammer that can be used by Christians to build Habitat for Humanity houses can be used by criminals to attack their victims.

Religious texts can be misinterpreted, to be sure. But medical texts can be misused by unscrupulous doctors. Physical laws governing explosives can be misused to destroy embassies. Airplanes can unite families or destroy buildings. The internet can be used to make an airplane bomb; is this the fault of Tim Berners-Lee, the inventor of the World Wide Web?

Philosopher Keith Ward: "It is not religion that causes intolerance. It is intolerance that uses religion to give alleged 'moral' support to the real cause of intolerance—hatred of those perceived or imagined to be oppressors or threats to one's own welfare."

Ward cites Machiavelli, who noted that "if you wish to be evil and to get away with it, you must take great care that you appear to be committed to morality and religion, to core values of great, even cosmic importance." Religion will continue to be used by evil people for their evil ends. Is this the fault of religion that it can be so misused? What about Nazi doctors who used medicine to "improve" the Aryan race through horrific experiments? As Ward notes, "There is no conceivable system of religious or political thought that has no potential dangers."

Writing for the *New York Times*, David Satter notes that "no fewer than 20 million Soviet citizens were put to death by the [Communist] regime or died as a direct result of its repressive policies." He adds: "If we add to this list the deaths caused by communist regimes that the Soviet Union created and supported—including those in Eastern Europe, China, Cuba, North Korea, Vietnam and Cambodia—the total number of victims is closer to 100 million."

Each was a victim of a government that was officially atheistic. Are we to blame all atheists for such atrocities?

Five: Religion is not to blame for the consequences of rejecting God.

Many of the problems that opponents of evangelical Christianity seek to blame on us are actually the result of rejecting the Lord we serve. Tony Evans perceptively notes:

> Freedom means you get to control the choice, but because God is the sovereign ruler over his creation, you don't get to control the consequences. He will rule by either endorsing your choice, or he will rule by allowing you to have the consequences of a decision made against him.
>
> For example, those who favor the legality of abortion on demand are making a choice against God's law not to take an innocent human being's life. God has given people the freedom to disobey him in making this choice antithetical to what he says. . . .
>
> There is a price tag for legalizing the shedding of innocent blood. The more unborn babies are murdered in our land, the more we can expect violence in our culture as well. Because when a culture goes against God's laws, God will allow that culture to experience the consequences of the breaking of that law—in this case the resultant devaluing of life as well as the effects of that devaluing.

We could cite other examples: the rejection of biblical sexuality and the resulting epidemics of pornography, sex trafficking, sexually transmitted diseases, and broken homes and lives; the promotion of euthanasia and the resulting devaluation of the elderly and the infirm; the unfettered use of technological and scientific capacities and the rising specter of designer babies and eugenics.

Erwin Lutzer writes: "It is said that after God died in the nineteenth century, man died in the twentieth. For when God is dead, man becomes an untamed beast."

If we reject God and his word, those who seek to honor him and obey his word are not to blame for the consequences.

The good Christianity does

Not only is the claim that "religion is dangerous" illogical and fallacious, the good that religion has done across its history shows that it is wrong on the merits as well.

The positive contributions of religion

Psychologists have long known that being religious, rather than harming adherents, actually helps them find greater happiness. For instance, a psychology professor named Catherine Sanderson has concluded that religious beliefs "give people a sense of meaning" and "a sense of well-being or comfort." Being religious often engages us in social networks that bring significance and belonging. And it is good for those who engage in it.

According to *U.S. News & World Report*, "There is overwhelming research evidence that people can live longer if they actively engage in formal religious activities and follow their faith's behavioral prescriptions." As one sociologist stated, "Regular and frequent religious attendance does seem to be one of the significant predictors of less stress and more life satisfaction."

In Richard Dawkins's universe, there would be no Martin Luther King Jr., no Gandhi or Mother Teresa; no Mozart, Bach, Rubens, or Michelangelo; no Red Cross; no St. Francis or Jesus. Would this be a less dangerous or more dangerous world?

The positive contributions of Christianity

Plato was convinced that a democracy could not last. The people could be swayed too easily by public speakers, he warned. And once the people discovered that they could vote based on their personal interests rather than the good of the nation, their democracy would begin to fail.

In a democracy, we do not seek to legislate morality. But did the Founders of our nation believe that morality was essential to their democratic experiment?

George Washington, in his 1796 Farewell Address, clearly asserted the need for religion in a moral society: "Of all the dispositions and habits which lead to political prosperity, religion and morality are indispensable supports. . . . Reason and experience both forbid us to expect that national morality can prevail in exclusion of religious principle. . . . Virtue or morality is a necessary spring of popular government."

Two years later, John Adams claimed that "our Constitution was made only for a moral and religious people. It is wholly inadequate to the government of any other." Adams also claimed that "the general principles on which the fathers achieved independence were . . . the general principles of Christianity." He also wrote in his diary entry for February 22, 1756: "Suppose a nation in some distant region should take the Bible for their only law book, and every member should regulate his conduct by the precepts there exhibited! Every member would be obliged in conscience, to temperance, frugality, and industry, to justice, kindness, and charity towards his fellow men; and to piety, love, and reverence toward Almighty God. What a Eutopia, what a Paradise would this region be."

Thomas Jefferson, our third president, was not a biblical Christian. He cut from the Bible every reference to the miraculous and viewed Jesus as only a man. But he insisted, "Injustice in government undermines the foundations of a society. A nation, therefore, must take measures to encourage its members along the paths of justice and morality."

And Abraham Lincoln addressed the Bible Society in Springfield, Illinois, with this description of God's word: "It seems to me that nothing short of infinite wisdom could by any possibility have devised and given to man this excellent and perfect moral code. It is suited to men in all the conditions of life and inculcates all the duties they owe to their Creator, to themselves, and to their fellow men."

The Founders knew that democracy requires morality, a basic insistence on character and integrity by the culture. Returning to such a conviction is essential to our survival and future as a nation.

Keith Ward adds:

> The church did preserve ancient classical culture in times of chaos and anarchy. It inspired the building of great cathedrals and sublime works of art in icons, mosaics, and illuminated manuscripts. In its monasteries it gave rise to traditions of scholarship and philosophical debate, as well as helping to build a sound agricultural economy and a refuge for those seeking a sense of the presence of God. And in ordinary life it campaigned for hospitality for strangers, care for the sick, education for all, and the preaching of love, compassion, and hope in a world darkened by plague, disease, the cruelty of war, and early death. These quotidian mercies are hugely positive factors that are largely hidden from the eyes of those historians who notice only the grand movements of the rich and powerful. But they are where we might expect to find the most positive fruits of a religion that has always claimed to speak most of all to the poor and every day and to let its works of charity be performed in secret, silently.

C. S. Lewis noted:

> If you read history, you will find that the Christians who did the most for the present

world were just those who thought most of the next. The Apostles themselves, who set on foot the conversion of the Roman Empire, the great men who built up the Middle Ages, the English Evangelicals who abolished the slave trade, all left their mark on earth, precisely because their minds were occupied with heaven. It is since Christians have largely ceased to think of the other world that they have become so ineffective in this. Aim at heaven and you will get earth "thrown in": aim at earth and you will get neither.

Jesus taught his followers to feed the hungry, clothe the naked, care for the sick, and visit the imprisoned, knowing that we will receive heavenly reward for such earthly service (Matthew 25:31–40). Around the world, his followers are doing what he asked.

In *Jesus Skeptic: A Journalist Explores the Credibility and Impact of Christianity*, John S. Dickerson notes that nine of the ten best nations on earth for women's rights, according to the World Economic Forum, have majority Christian populations.

Followers of Jesus such as Isaac Newton, Johannes Kepler, and Blaise Pascal also played an essential role in launching the Scientific Revolution. According to Dickerson, "These great scientists who unlocked the Scientific Revolution . . . were not incidentally Christian. They were not accidentally Christian. They did not happen to be Christian. Their whole way of seeing the world and the universe was through the lens of Jesus as God, a real being who they firmly believed in. They believed Jesus to be God who is good and who works with order and predictability." Dickerson adds that "nearly every leading university in the world was founded by Christians" and notes that hospitals and formal philanthropy to care for the poor grew largely from Christian ministries.

He notes, "In my examination of the influential abolitionists who led the American populace to overthrow slavery, I have yet to find one who was not a Christian." He also states, "Remove Christians from the last five hundred years, and the evidence suggests we would be much closer to the illiterate average people of world history. That is, without the Christian-founded norm of public education, the letters on this page would make no more sense to us than they do to a chipmunk."

An example from history

J. Edwin Orr, one of the great historians of spiritual awakening, wrote a now-classic essay titled "Prayer and Revival." He shows that in the wake of the American Revolution, the new nation slid into tragic moral decay. Drunkenness became epidemic—out of a population of five million, 300,000 were confirmed alcoholics; 15,000 of them died from drinking every year. Women were afraid of assault; banks were being robbed daily.

The churches were in serious decline. Methodists, Baptists, and Presbyterians all lost more members than they gained. One Congregational church did not see a new member for sixteen years. An Episcopal bishop resigned his post since he had not confirmed anyone in so many years that he determined he no longer had a ministry to fulfill.

The Chief Justice of the United States, John Marshall, wrote to James Madison that the church "was too far gone ever to be redeemed." Tom Paine predicted that "Christianity will be forgotten in thirty years."

A poll at Harvard University found not a single believer there. A similar poll at Princeton discovered two Christians among the student body. Students held a mock communion at Williams College, staged anti-Christian plays at Dartmouth, and forced the resignation of Harvard's Christian president. Christians on campus in the 1790s were so few that they met in secret and kept their minutes in code.

What happened? Christians began to pray. Their prayer movement began in Great Britain under the leadership of William Carey, Andrew Fuller, and John Sutcliffe. In New England, a Baptist pastor named Isaac Backus issued an urgent plea for revival in the new nation. Churches set aside the first Monday of every month to pray. Other prayer meetings sprang up. A prayer network began to cross the land.

The result was the Second Great Awakening, a movement of God that created Sunday schools, Bible societies, popular education, and led to the abolition of slavery in England and eventually in America. Many historians say this Awakening was critical to the preservation of the United States.

A word about political engagement

I will argue in the next chapter that God is calling more Christians into public service than are answering his call. It is my adamant belief that we should be engaged in the political arena as in all other arenas of our society.

However, evangelical engagement with secular politics has sometimes undermined our witness more than it has advanced God's kingdom. For example, later in Billy Graham's career, the evangelist famously regretted some of his political statements and public alignments with political leaders.

In many ways, the evangelical association with political leaders and parties reached its zenith with the presidential campaign and administration of Donald Trump. Many evangelicals supported Mr. Trump in response to his endorsement of evangelical values such as the sanctity of life and the importance of religious freedom. His pledge to nominate only conservatives to the Supreme Court was instrumental as well.

However, many in secular society have seen evangelical support for Mr. Trump's positions on some issues as unconditional support for all he has said and done. If they disagree with his personal behavior and actions, they are likely to disagree with those they see as endorsing what they reject.

In the aftermath of the Capitol riots on January 6, 2021, evangelical theologian Ed Stetzer was asked what Mr. Trump has "done to the evangelical movement." His response: "If you asked today, 'What is an evangelical?' to most people, I would want them to say: someone who believes Jesus died on the cross for our sin and in our place and we're supposed to tell everyone about it. But for most people they'd say, 'Oh, those are those people who are really super supportive of the president no matter what he does.' And I don't think that's what we want to be known for."

Columnist Matt Lewis, who is himself a Christian, writes: "The connection between Christianity and the Republican Party has existed for four decades. But it's fair to say that associating religious faith with Ronald Reagan's sunny optimism or George W. Bush's 'compassionate conservatism' does not result in the same level of negative repercussions as embracing the MAGA ethos."

Lewis cites research indicating that the rise of Americans who identify as "nonreligious" can be correlated with a backlash against the Christian Right. He quotes one scholar who noted the widespread belief "that religion and the Republican Party go together, and that if you're not sympathetic to the Republican Party, you don't want anything to do with religion."

I believe Christians should participate fully in our political system. At the same time, we must be very discerning in guarding our witness and the larger message of the gospel.

Billy Graham testified: "I came close to identifying the American way of life with the kingdom of God. Then I realized that God had called me to a higher kingdom than America. I have tried to be faithful to my calling as a minister of the gospel."

We must do the same.

The Christian response to persecution

Let's consider one more factor: the biblical response to those who threaten us shows that our faith is not dangerous but redemptive. What is this response?

Expect persecution

Evangelicals expect to suffer for our faith. Jesus was clear:

- "If the world hates you, know that it has hated me before it hated you" (John 15:18).

- "If you were of the world, the world would love you as its own; but because you are not of the world, but I chose you out of the world, therefore the world hates you" (John 15:19).

- "They will deliver you up to tribulation and put you to death, and you will be hated by all nations for my name's sake" (Matthew 24:9).

The apostles agreed:

- John taught us, "Do not be surprised, brothers, that the world hates you" (1 John 3:13).

- Paul warned us, "All who desire to live a godly life in Christ Jesus will be persecuted" (2 Timothy 3:12).

- Peter encouraged us, "Beloved, do not be surprised at the fiery trial when it comes upon you to test you, as though something strange were happening to you" (1 Peter 4:12).

As many as two million Christians were killed in the first centuries of the Christian faith. My youth minister used to say, if you and the devil aren't running into each other, you're probably running with each other. But it's easy to think that this cannot be true for us, that we will not have to pay such a price for our faith.

One reason is that Americans have been conditioned to experience life as consumers. Philosopher Chad Engelland is right: "Our waking lives more and more resemble a never-ending all-you-can-eat buffet. Consumables include movies, books, music, stuff—with Amazon Prime, Spotify Premium, Netflix, and YouTube among others treating us to an unending smorgasbord of consumption. There's content, lots of it, and free with a paid subscription, making it hard not to binge-watch, which is but the latest form of our binge-buying and binge-consuming."

In our culture, you and I are in charge. We are told that we can have what we want when we want it. However, the reality is different: "Your adversary the devil prowls around like a roaring lion, seeking someone to devour" (1 Peter 5:8). Note the present tense.

Another factor is that you and I have been living in an unusual period in history. For most of my lifetime, evangelicals have been empowered on a significant level in American culture. We have helped to elect presidents, pass legislation, and advance our beliefs. We have seen the birth and growth of megachurches across the land. It's been easy to think that this is the way it has always been and will always be.

However, as we have seen, those days are ending.

Love and pray for those who persecute us

When we face persecution, Jesus' instruction is simple: "Love your enemies and pray for those who persecute you" (Matthew 5:44). Consider each imperative in turn.

- "Love" translates *agape*, the unconditional commitment to put another person first. It is a present active imperative verb, literally "love and keep on loving."

- "Enemies" translates *echthrous*, "one who is at war with you." Why should we love such people? Because enemies of our faith can resist our logic, ignore our sermons, and boycott our services, but they have no defense for unconditional love.

- "Pray" translates *proseuchesthe*, a present active imperative that could be translated as "pray and keep on praying."

- "Those who persecute you" translates *diokonton*, "those who are seeking to drive you out." Pray continually for those who persecute you, even as they persecute you.

Then God does what we cannot do. Human words cannot change human hearts. Only the Spirit can convict of sin and save souls. Only he can make Saul the persecutor into Paul the apostle. Only he can turn enemies of God into disciples of Jesus.

Craig Denison writes: "Blessing those who have hurt you is one of the hardest things to do as a believer. It requires the perspective and fortitude to choose God's ways over what feels most gratifying at the time. But you have the power to choose the abundant life God makes available to you in every moment. The Holy Spirit will help you forgive and offer grace to others if you will allow him to. Choose to bless those who persecute you today, and watch as the love and honor you show others brings heaven to earth around you."

Utilize the legal system to protect our religious rights

Scripture warns us, "Beloved, never avenge yourselves, but leave it to the wrath of God" (Romans 12:19). Jesus taught us, "Do not resist the one who is evil. But if anyone slaps you on the right cheek, turn to him the other also" (Matthew 5:39). Paul warned Christians that bringing lawsuits against believers harms our witness before unbelievers (1 Corinthians 6:1–8).

At the same time, Scripture teaches, "You shall not pervert the justice due to your poor in his lawsuit" (Exodus 23:6). When Paul was about to be whipped by a Roman centurion, he asked, "Is it lawful for you to flog a man who is a Roman citizen and uncondemned?" (Acts 22:25).

He appealed to his Roman citizenship in Philippi as well to clear himself and his fellow Christians from legal jeopardy (Acts 16:37–39). When he stood trial before Festus in Caesarea, he appealed to Caesar (Acts 25:12). In each case, he utilized the legal system of the day to appeal injustice and advance his ministry.

Several organizations exist to help Christians do the same today. First Liberty, the Alliance Defending Freedom, and the Becket Fund are three with which I am very familiar. I highly recommend them to believers whose religious freedoms are being attacked.

Often, corporate organizations do not know where the courts have drawn boundaries in this context. Christians have expansive religious freedoms in our society. We should use the means at our disposal to proclaim God's word and advance his kingdom.

Redeeming the attack on biblical Christians

At its heart, persecution against evangelicals is an attack of the Enemy. Jesus warned that Satan was "a murderer from the beginning" (John 8:44), a thief who "comes only to steal and kill and destroy" (John 10:10). It is no coincidence that persecution is increasing fastest in those regions where the church is growing most rapidly. But Scripture assures us that "he who is in you is greater than he who is in the world" (1 John 4:4).

God redeems all he allows. His holy character requires him to redeem for greater good everything he allows or causes. In this case, he uses persecution to purify and strengthen his people. Tertullian, one of the early church fathers, famously noted that the blood of the martyrs is the seed of the church. If we respond to such opposition by speaking the truth in love, he uses our response to advance his kingdom.

During my first visit to Cuba, I told one of the pastors that I was praying for persecution to lessen against his people. He asked me not to pray in this way since he and other pastors believed that the suffering they faced was vital to their spiritual health and purity. Then he confided that he and other Cubans were praying for persecution against Christians to increase in America for the same reason.

Christophe Munzihirwa was the Roman Catholic Archbishop of Bukavu in eastern Zaire. He was assassinated by a group of Rwandan soldiers on October 29, 1996. At his funeral, someone quoted his favorite saying: "There are things that can be seen only with eyes that have cried."

As God uses the suffering of his people to strengthen their faith, more of us will see more than we have ever seen before.

Early Christians showed the Roman world the relevance of their faith by demonstrating its positive results in their personal lives and public ministry. For example, they had no political power to abolish slavery, so they purchased slaves and freed them. They could not end the horrific practice of abandoning unwanted babies, so they rescued discarded babies and raised them as their own.

This is why Justin Martyr (ca. AD 100–165) could say of his fellow Christians, "We who hated and destroyed one another, and on account of their different manners would not live with men of a different tribe, now, since the coming of Christ, live familiarly with them, and pray for our enemies." An early Christian named Minucius Felix testified to the Romans, "We love one another . . . with a mutual love, because we do not know how to hate."

In a culture famed for its violence and barbarism, the transforming grace of Christ was a powerful apologetic for the gospel of Christ. When we respond to attacks with compassion and to hate with love, we show a skeptical culture this grace at work.

The darker the room, the more powerful the light.

"Contend for the faith that was once for all delivered to the saints."
—JUDE 3

Conclusion:
How to be the change
we wish to see

My wife and I have often said that if we could live two lives, one of them would be in Hawaii. A few times over the decades of our marriage, we have saved up enough airline miles to fly to this Pacific paradise. Each time, we are astonished by the natural beauty we encounter.

However, there is one aspect of nature in Hawaii that I could do without: tsunamis.

Travelers see tsunami signs around the islands and especially near the coasts, warning of possible tsunamis and marking the way to shelters. Such preparations are essential: since 1812, Hawaii has experienced 135 confirmed tsunamis.

There are three large tsunami sources near the islands, but the islands are also in the crosshairs of distant tsunamis generated from South America (19 percent), Kamchatka and Kuril Islands (16 percent), the West Coast of North and Central America (13 percent), Alaska and the Aleutian Islands (13 percent), and the South Pacific Islands and New Zealand (12 percent).

Nine tsunamis over the years caused 294 deaths; 245 of these deaths were from distant tsunami sources.

Hawaii's history with tsunamis illustrates our thesis: earthquakes we cannot see can generate tidal waves that can be deadly. Knowing when the tsunami is coming is vital to avoiding its dangerous effects.

Dr. Albert Mohler is convinced that Christians are facing such a threat today: "We are living in the midst of a revolution. The Christian church in the West now faces a set of challenges that exceeds anything it has experienced in the past. The revolution that has transformed most of Western Europe and much of North America is a revolution more subtle and more dangerous than revolutions faced in previous generations. This is a revolution of ideas—one that is transforming the entire moral structure of meaning and life that human beings have recognized for millennia."

In the face of such a threat, it is obviously vital for Christians to prepare, to know where to find the shelters that we need. But I also want to assert that it is vital for us to do what we can to stop this tsunami before it reaches its full devastation.

Stopping the tsunami

Usama Kadri is a mathematician with the University of Cardiff in the UK. He believes he has discovered a way to stop tsunamis before they reach land by using the pressure of deep-ocean sound waves.

Specifically, he advocates the use of acoustic-gravity waves (AGWs). He states that such waves occur naturally in the oceans, cutting through the water at the speed of sound. He believes that controlling them could give us a way to reduce a tsunami's momentum by diluting its strength so that most of its energy would be dissipated before it reaches land. If such waves could be engineered and controlled, death and chaos could be lessened enormously.

As with our oceans, so with our nation.

I am convinced that it is not too late for Christians to respond redemptively to the cultural tsunami we have discussed in this book. As we have seen, we can:

- Defend biblical truth and redeem this "earthquake" by demonstrating the truth and relevance of God's word in our lives.

- Defend biblical morality and redeem this "earthquake" by demonstrating courageous compassion to LGBTQ individuals, women considering abortion, and others affected by the sexual revolution.

- Defend biblical equality and redeem this "earthquake" by building relational bridges across racial divides leading to transformational community.

- Defend biblical Christians and redeem this "earthquake" by demonstrating the positive value of Christianity for the common good in our world and in our personal lives and influence.

In this concluding chapter, we'll discuss practical ways to live and act with such redemptive engagement and grace.

Christ transforming culture

I predict that evangelicals will respond to escalating cultural opposition in five ways, adapted from Richard Niebuhr's classic book *Christ and Culture:*

Christ of culture: Some will modify their beliefs in alignment with the shifting cultural tide. As we have noted, we are already watching pastors and theologians "change their minds" on biblical sexual morality. This approach jettisons foundational biblical truth in a never-ending quest for cultural relevance.

Christ against culture: Some will demonize those who disagree with them and characterize the "other side" as the enemy. Others will withdraw from social engagement into communities where they can practice their faith without opposition. They will keep the "light" of the gospel under their "basket" while repelling those who might be attracted to it (Matthew 5:14–16).

Christ above culture: Some will adhere to biblical morality when in community with fellow Christians but make culturally required concessions in their secular lives and work. They may be able to avoid the consequences of their private beliefs, but their public compromises will hinder their witness and grieve their Lord.

Christ and culture in paradox: Some will engage secular society in order to defend religious liberty, working to secure a minority position for evangelicals in culture. This is a valuable and urgent mission, but we must do more than seek the "right to be wrong."

Christ transforming culture: Some will speak biblical truth with courageous compassion. They will declare and defend biblical morality because they know that its truth is best for all people. They will view those who reject God's word as those who most need God's word. "Speaking the truth in love" will be their mantra and their mission (Ephesians 4:15).

This is clearly the most biblical and effective way to respond to rising cultural opposition.

You and I are living in a Daniel 6 moment where we are called to worship the secular rather than the spiritual and must choose to be faithful regardless of the consequences. We should remember that God did not deliver his prophet until he was in the lions' den. Daniel had to be faithful to the end.

As with Daniel, so with us: God promises that his will for us is "good and acceptable and perfect" (Romans 12:2). You probably know that your Father has a will for where you live, that it was his plan for you to be where you are today. But did you know that he also has a will for *when* you live? By his providence, you were not alive a century ago or a century from now (if the Lord tarries). He knew that with his help, you could meet the challenges of this day. Otherwise, you would not be alive to face them (cf. 1 Corinthians 10:13).

You are one of his missionaries to a culture more opposed to faith than any in American history. You are called to love and pray for this culture. You are called to prove your faith by your love, to earn the right to share the gospel. And you are called to pray urgently, passionately, daily for the great spiritual awakening we so desperately need. This is the need of the hour, and you are called to meet it. How?

Model Christlike civility

New York Times columnist Ross Douthat penned one of the most perceptive analyses I have seen of this moment in our cultural history. In *Bad Religion: How We Became A Nation of Heretics*, he tells the story of America's long engagement with religion. He describes the days when Christianity was an assumed and foundational part of American culture and notes with personal sadness that this role is waning, if not over.

However, he claims that it is too soon for Christians to give up on making a difference in our culture. He suggests that a faith which engages our post-Christian society effectively must be political without being partisan, ecumenical but also confessional, moralistic but also holistic. He adds: "It is not enough for Americans to respect orthodox Christianity a bit more than they do at present. To make any difference in our common life, Christianity must be *lived*—not as a means to social cohesion or national renewal, but as an end unto itself. Anyone who seeks a more perfect union should begin by seeking the perfection of their own soul."

You and I are called to speak the truth in love (Ephesians 4:15), standing boldly but graciously for our Lord and his people. When our faith is attacked, God wants us to "make a defense to anyone who asks you for a reason for the hope that is in you" (1 Peter 3:15a).

However, we are to make this defense "with gentleness and respect, having a good conscience, so that, when you are slandered, those who revile your good behavior in Christ may be put to shame" (vs. 15b–16). Then the apostle adds: "It is better to suffer for doing good, if that should be God's will, than for doing evil" (v. 17).

Phil Cooke is a filmmaker, media consultant, and author. He observed:

> The great challenge of the Church today is speaking into a culture that perceives us as an irrelevant, out of touch museum piece. . . . The Christian Church has to come to terms with the fact that while its role in leading American culture may be over, its voice at the table is not. That doesn't mean we side-step issues that matter, but we speak the truth in a way that engages rather than condemns. In a media-driven culture, perception matters. Two thousand years ago, an obscure, marginal group following the teachings of Jesus became the dominant religious force in the Western world. They didn't have political power, an army, or vast wealth. But through their lifestyle, their relationships, and their actions, they changed the perception of Rome and eventually impacted the world.

John S. Dickerson is right: "We are not here to attack or fight our neighbors when they disagree with us; we are here to be diplomats and ambassadors to them."

Jesus taught us that if a person sins against us, we are to go to them (Matthew 18:15). Conversely, if we sin against others, we are to initiate reconciliation with them (Matthew 5:23–24). In other words, we are not allowed to talk *about* our opponents until we talk *to* them. Slander is forbidden by the word and will of God (Psalm 101:5).

However, it is impossible for us consistently to be the people of civility our culture needs apart from the power of God operating in and through our lives.

In my book *Respectfully, I Disagree: How to Be a Civil Person in an Uncivil Time*, I encourage Christians to be people of civility. Here's how: begin every day by submitting our lives to the Holy Spirit (Ephesians 5:18) and practice the spiritual disciplines that position us to experience God's best. As a result, we will manifest the fruit of the Spirit to the world (Galatians 5:22–23).

Use your influence for God's kingdom

Sociologist James Davison Hunter has advanced a theory of cultural change that I find enormously persuasive. In *To Change the World*, he writes that culture changes "top down" as individuals achieve their highest place of influence and live there faithfully. Dr. Hunter calls this "manifesting faithful presence."

Consider four practical ways to do this.

One: Identify your missional calling.

Every Christian has a kingdom assignment, a way of advancing God's kingdom that is uniquely theirs. To identify yours:

- Identify your spiritual gifts. For help, I invite you to take my online spiritual gifts analysis at denisonforum.org.

- Define your personal passions. Frederick Buechner noted, "The place God calls you to is the place where your deep gladness and the world's deep hunger meet."

- Ask trusted friends to help you determine your best ways to serve.

- Note open and closed doors.

- Ask the Lord for his guidance: "If any of you lacks, wisdom, let him ask God, who gives generously to all without reproach, and it will be given him" (James 1:5). The prophet promised, "Your ears shall hear a word behind you, saying, 'This is the way, walk in it,' when you turn to the right or when you turn to the left" (Isaiah 30:21).

But always remember that your highest calling is not to your culture but to your Lord. Anthony Esolen is right:

> Love does not hoard itself up but gives freely, gives with abandon; so that he who seeks first of all to save his life shall lose it, but he who is willing to lose his life shall save it. The corollary for culture and civilization is clear enough. You cannot save a culture by raising culture to the ultimate good. . . .
>
> Cut off from the springs of the divine, the best that has been thought and said loses all conviction, and the best that has been done seems impossible ever to do again. . . . He who would save a culture or a civilization must not seek first the culture or the civilization, but the kingdom of God, and then all these other things, says Jesus, shall be given to him as well.

Two: Serve with discernment.

Christians in business or political leadership are especially trusted with cultural influence. As with all believers, they should consider these opportunities to be their missionary assignment.

However, discernment is obviously necessary. Jesus sends us out "as sheep in the midst of wolves, so be wise as serpents and innocent as doves" (Matthew 10:16). Corporate and political leaders need to know where legal and corporate lines exist with regard to their personal beliefs and public statements. They should take actions that cross such lines only if they are clearly called to do so by our Lord and are willing to pay the price.

And they should never minimize the influence of their personal lives and character. An executive with a Bible on her desk, a corporate leader known to spend time in personal prayer, and a CEO who volunteers personal time to help those in need are examples of being the "light of the world" and the "salt of the earth" (Matthew 5:13–16).

Three: Consider public service.

As I stated earlier, I am convinced that God is calling more Christians into public service than are answering his call.

Joseph served as prime minister of Egypt (Genesis 41:40–44). Mordecai rose to "second in rank to King Ahasuerus" (Esther 10:3). Nicodemus (John 7:50–51) and Joseph of Arimathea (Luke 23:50) both served in the Sanhedrin, the Supreme Court of first-century Israel.

The Roman emperor Constantine (272–337) ended centuries of persecution by legalizing the Christian faith. Justinian I (482–565) developed a legal code in which he embedded much that was unapologetically Christian and had twenty-five churches erected in Constantinople alone. Queen Elizabeth I (1533–1603) was "a woman of strong faith who recognized her own vulnerabilities and who embraced utterly the basic tenets of Reformation theology."

William Wilberforce led the fight to abolish the slave trade in England primarily because his Christian faith moved him with courageous compassion for its victims. As we have seen, many of America's founding fathers were committed Christians who sought to lead and live by biblical principles.

But note: electing Christians to office is not enough.

As a result of the Watergate scandal, Nixon administration official Chuck Colson served time in prison, where he became a follower of Jesus and one of the most perceptive cultural commentators in America. He noted: "American politics simply mirrors the loss of character in the American people. If citizens are not willing to put the civic good above their own, they can't expect their leaders to do it for them. In this way, by eroding our sense of societal responsibility, radical individualism paves the way for the death of community."

We need to serve in public office or pray and support those who do (1 Timothy 2:1–2).

Four: Use your personal platforms to promote your values.

I have been privileged to pastor a number of Christians in public service. Without fail, they have told me that most citizens have no idea the influence they can have with their elected officials. A single letter or email is magnified by hundreds or thousands by those who receive it in the belief that many more people probably agree with the person who is writing.

Appearing at a school board meeting or city council hearing carries great weight. Developing personal relationships with elected officials is a very effective way to advance our beliefs and worldview with them.

Consumers can have significant influence with companies as well through economic and social media strategies. I am not necessarily a supporter of boycotts since it can be difficult to marshal enough financial response to make a meaningful difference and such actions typically hurt employees of the company more than the leaders making the decisions we are protesting. In addition, they position us in the culture as "haters" more than "lovers," showing what we are against rather than what we are for.

However, there can be times when companies act in ways that require an economic response, both negative and positive. For example, when Chick-fil-A was targeted several years ago by LGBTQ activists, Christians organized a day when believers were encouraged to buy food from the restaurant chain. By contrast, many Christians have chosen no longer to shop at Target after the store announced its transgender-friendly bathroom policy.

In addition, Christians can use their social media platforms to make public their support or disapproval of business agendas and decisions. Of course, we must always use such platforms in ways that honor our Lord and draw people to him. As we have seen, civility is vital as we speak the truth in love (Ephesians 4:15).

Eight beatitudes for culture-changing Christians

In his bestselling book *Cultural Literacy: What Every American Needs to Know*, E. D. Hirsch Jr. stated, "To be culturally literate is to possess the basic information needed to thrive in the modern world." My purpose in writing this book has been to define and describe some basic information needed to *change* the world.

To that end, let's close with this good news: the twenty-first century will look more like the first century than any in between. In apostolic Christianity, the church possessed no buildings or recognized clergy. They worked in a culture that had no generally accepted definition of truth. They persecuted Christians by the thousands and eventually the millions. But they soon became the largest spiritual movement in human history.

Here's how: They did their work by relevance. They showed a skeptical culture the love of God by their love. They adopted abandoned babies, bought and freed slaves, befriended prostitutes, cared for lepers, and prayed for their persecutors. When they fed hungry bodies, they fed hungry souls. They proved the relevance and reality of their faith by their love.

So can we, if we will do what they did.

Let's close with eight "beatitudes" as a code of values that can motivate and empower us to be the culture-changing Christians our society needs so desperately today.

One: Be yielded.

In 1988, Yale historian Paul Kennedy wrote *The Rise and Fall of the Great Powers*. His thesis has been much discussed: Nations ascend due to the supremacy of their material resources; they inevitably spend their wealth on military expansion to maintain their power; and they fall into decline and eventual collapse. The Roman Empire is usually cited as Exhibit A of Kennedy's thesis.

It's easy to see why many people link America to Rome.

We attained global superpower status after World War II and sole superpower status after the end of the Cold War and the collapse of the Soviet Union. We invested in military expansion to fight Communism in South Korea and Vietnam and to fight jihadism in Afghanistan, Iraq, and Syria. Along the way, we encountered the 2008 Great Recession and the 2020 Great Pandemic. We are witnessing the rise of China and the rising threat of Russia. As I write, we are watching conflict again in the Middle East and a growing immigration crisis on our southern border. We are embroiled daily in political division and bitter rancor. It seems that America's greatest days are behind her.

In *Are We Rome?: The Fall of an Empire and the Fate of America*, Cullen Murphy notes a variety of similarities between their empire and ours: what he calls "military overstretch," the tendency of "global myopia" (underestimating threats in the distance), and the "curse of empire" (the inherent instability of large systems).

I would add a fourth factor: transactional religion.

The Romans worshiped distant gods who lived atop Mount Olympus in a kind of business arrangement. They placed sacrifices on the altars of their gods so the gods would answer their prayers. If you were going to war, you sacrificed to Mars; if you sought wisdom, you sacrificed to Athena. You did your job, and they would do theirs. They lived with a clear separation between the spiritual and the secular, between religion and the "real world."

American religion functions in the same way: go to church on Sunday so God will bless you on Monday; start your day with Bible study and prayer so God will bless your day; give money so God will bless your money.

Christianity, however, is not a transactional religion but a transformational relationship.

As we have seen, Jesus calls the person who would be his disciple to "deny himself and take up his cross daily and follow me" (Luke 9:23). We are told to "present your bodies as a living sacrifice" to God (Romans 12:1), to be "crucified with Christ" (Galatians 2:20).

God wants to be king of every dimension of our lives, every moment of our lives. He can lead only those who will follow and give what we will receive. To experience the abundant life of Jesus (John 10:10), we must "abide" fully in Jesus (John 15:5a). Otherwise, Jesus warns us, "apart from me you can do nothing" (v. 5b).

This is why, as we have noted, we should begin every day by submitting our day and lives to our Lord (Ephesians 5:18). And why we should stay yielded to his Spirit all through our day so that he can do through us what we could never do for him.

Peter Kreeft effectively describes the culture wars of our generation, then concludes with a chapter titled "The Secret Weapon That Will Win the War." What is it? Saints.

He explains: "The strongest weapon in the world is sanctity. Nothing can defeat it." For evidence, he points to the apostolic Christians who sparked the Christian movement that is now more than two billion strong. He points to "the double devotion to truth and love" that they embodied and identifies it as "the only weapon that can win the war against the culture of death."

As a result, he concludes, "Only saints can save the world."

What is keeping us from being saints? Kreeft quotes this convicting statement from William Law's *Serious Call to a Devout and Holy Life*: "If you will look into your own heart in utter honesty, you must admit that there is one and only one reason why you are not, even now, as saintly as the primitive Christians: you do not wholly want to be."

Do you "wholly want to be"?

Two: Be aware.

In his classic book *The Naked Public Square*, Richard John Neuhaus warned, "We are neophiliacs, lovers of the new who are titillated by the news. It gives us an illusory sense of involvement in our times. We fear being left out of what is happening. The imperative of participation, carried to excess, becomes frenetic and compulsive."

He wrote these words in 1984. What would he say of our 24/7/365 digital age and its social media compulsions?

While the news can be overwhelming, retreating from culture is not an option for God's people. Christians must resist the temptation to withdraw from the world, choosing instead to take Christ to all nations as fervently and effectively as possible (Matthew 28:19).

The prophets of the Old Testament clearly and consistently spoke out against the cultural sins of their day. For example, Hosea condemned the "swearing, lying, murder, stealing, and committing adultery" of his culture (Hosea 4:2). He also warned his society against drunkenness and sexual immorality (4:18) as well.

Amos condemned enslavement (Amos 1:6–8), mistreatment of pregnant women (1:13) and the poor (2:6), sexual abuse (2:7), drunkenness (4:1), greed (5:11), and corruption (5:12). Obadiah warned against violence (Obadiah 10); Micah condemned theft (Micah 2:1–2).

Much like the prophets of old, Paul was grieved by idolatry (Acts 17:16) and the sins of his day, many of which he listed specifically (Romans 1:18–32; Galatians 5:19–21). He had "great sorrow and unceasing anguish in [his] heart" (Romans 9:2) for his fellow Jews who had not made Jesus their Messiah. And he gave his life as a missionary to the Gentile world (Galatians 2:7–8).

Know what is happening and why, on this issue and others affecting our faith and culture.

Three: Be urgent.

The brilliant urbanologist Jane Jacobs warned: "A culture is unsalvageable if stabilizing forces themselves become ruined and irrelevant. This is what I fear for our own culture."

John Winthrop (1588–1649) helped establish the Massachusetts Bay Colony, then he served as governor of the settlement for twelve of its first twenty years. In his address in 1630 to passengers aboard the ship *Arbella*, bound for the New World, he famously stated: "We must consider that we shall be as a city upon a hill. The eyes of all people are upon us. So that if we shall deal falsely with our God in this work we have undertaken, and so cause him to withdraw his present help from us, we shall be made a story and a byword through the world."

Winthrop further warned his fellow colonists of the dangers that lay ahead if they turned from their commitment to Christ: "If our hearts shall turn away, so that we will not obey, but shall be seduced, and worship other gods, our pleasure and profits, and serve them; it is propounded unto us this day, we shall surely perish out of the good land whither we pass over this vast sea to possess it. Therefore, let us choose life, that we and our seed may live, by obeying his voice and cleaving to him, for he is our life and our prosperity."

As we have seen, American culture is turning away from the one true God to "worship other gods, our pleasure and profits, and serve them." Winthrop is right: a holy God must judge that which is unrepentantly ungodly.

The hour is late.

Four: Be compassionate.

Novelist Walker Percy observed: "By remaining faithful to its original commission, by serving its people with love, especially the poor, the lonely, and the disposed, and by not surrendering its doctrinal steadfastness, sometimes even the very contradiction of culture by which it serves as a sign, surely the Church serves the culture best."

Earlier we noted 2 Corinthians 4:4: "The god of this world has blinded the minds of the unbelievers, to keep them from seeing the light of the gospel of the glory of Christ." As a result, unbelievers and others who oppose biblical truth are deceived. They are not the enemy—Satan is the enemy.

President Ronald Reagan admonished those who served in his administration, "Remember, we have no enemies, only opponents."

Randel Everett is right: "It is important to get the idea of God right because we inevitably become like the god we worship. If we worship an immoral god, we become lewd in our behavior. If we worship an arbitrary, hostile god, we become angry and antagonistic. If our god is a legalistic, demanding, and harsh god, we also become legalistic, demanding, and harsh. If we worship a sentimental god, then we become emotional in our approach to god and to others in life. We become like the god we worship."

French philosopher Étienne Gilson warned: "There still remains only God to protect man against man. Either we will serve him in spirit and in truth or we shall enslave ourselves ceaselessly, more and more, to the monstrous idol that we have made with our own hands to our own image and likeness."

Because people in our secularized culture are enslaving themselves to this "monstrous idol," they deserve our compassion rather than our condemnation, our humble ministry rather than our elitist rejection.

Many years ago, a famous pastor in Dallas, Texas, made headlines when his involvement in a number of sexual affairs came to light. The next week, I attended chapel at Southwestern Baptist Theological Seminary, where I served on faculty. The speaker for the service began his sermon by describing the news reports in some detail. I assumed he was going to condemn the pastor for his immorality and the shame he had brought on his church and the Church.

I was wrong.

After reporting on the pastor's sins, the speaker pointed his finger at us and said, "And there but for the grace of God go you." Then he pointed at himself and added, "And there but for the grace of God go I."

The ground is level at the foot of the cross.

Five: Be engaged.

In his cultural engagement, Paul followed the example and ministry of our Lord. Jesus fed the hungry (John 6:1–14), healed the sick (Mark 1:33–34), and befriended the outcast (Luke 19:1–10).

Our Lord taught us to do the same, calling us to be "salt" and "light" (Matthew 5:13–16). Both transform all they contact. As a result, the first Christians gave their goods to anyone who "had need" (Acts 2:45) and ministered to "the sick and those afflicted with unclean spirits" (Acts 5:16).

Clearly, they did more than "preach the gospel." Or, better said, they preached the gospel of God's love in actions as well as in words. They met felt need in order to meet spiritual need, earning the right to share the message of salvation in Christ.

We can do the same as the Lord leads and empowers us.

Six: Be courageous.

I read each day from *A Diary of Private Prayer* by the Scottish theologian and minister John Baillie. I recently prayed these words he suggested: "Make me wise today to see all things within the dimension of eternity and make me brave to face all the changes in my life that come from this vision." This is a prayer I believe our Lord delights to answer and a prayer we need to pray daily.

Erwin W. Lutzer writes: "Recently, a volunteer here at Moody Church told us that in her daughter's school students were asked to choose sides in a classroom. On one side were the students who claimed to be gay and those who supported their lifestyle. On the other side were the bullies. Now, her daughter was forced to decide: should she join the bullies, or should she walk over and endorse the gay lifestyle?"

He comments: "The day of casual Christianity is over. No longer is it possible to drift along, hoping that no tough choices will have to be made. At this point in American history, any moral and spiritual progress will have to be won at great cost. The darker the night, the more important every candle becomes."

As Joshua was about to face enemies who would seek to destroy him and his people, the Lord said to him, "Be strong and courageous.

Do not be frightened, and do not be dismayed, for the LORD your God is with you wherever you go" (Joshua 1:9). Paul encouraged early Christians to "be watchful, stand firm in the faith, act like men, be strong" (1 Corinthians 16:13).

Such strength comes from the One who meets all our needs according to his riches in glory (Philippians 4:19). If we will ask him for the courage we need when we need it, he will answer our prayer to his glory and our good.

I have been privileged to teach doctoral seminars for Dallas Baptist University at Oxford University several times over the years. We always make it a point to visit the Martyr's Memorial. It commemorates three Protestant martyrs: Thomas Cranmer, Nicholas Ridley, and Hugh Latimer. The three were burned at the stake near this location, Latimer and Ridley in 1555, Cranmer the next year.

As the flames rose around Latimer and Ridley, Latimer reportedly said to his fellow martyr, "Be of good comfort, Master Ridley, and play the man! We shall this day light such a candle by God's grace, in England, as I trust never shall be put out."

I have taught the word of God at this very location. The candle they lit "never shall be put out."

Like them, you and I are called to shine that candle in our dark culture with grace and courage to the glory of God.

Seven: Be sacrificial.

Jesus likened his kingdom to "a grain of mustard seed that a man took and sowed in his field" (Matthew 13:31). He observed, "It is the smallest of all seeds, but when it has grown it is larger than all the garden plants and becomes a tree, so that the birds of the air come and make nests in its branches" (v. 32).

This is a word of encouragement for followers of Jesus that our efforts, while they may seem small, can bear an enormous harvest. But it is also a word of challenge and warning. As Shane Claiborne notes, "Mustard must be crushed, ground, broken in order for its power to be released."

We noted in chapter 4 that Christians are facing persecution around the world and increasingly in the West as well. If we would stand redemptively for biblical truth, we must be willing to pay the price. To this end, I encourage you to make preparations in three ways.

First, choose to pay the price of your convictions before the bill comes due.

Decide today that Jesus is your Lord and King and that you will do whatever is necessary to follow him. He always intended his followers to carry their cross "daily" (Luke 9:23), to be crucified with him (Galatians 2:20), to surrender their lives as a "living sacrifice" (Romans 12:1). Determine now to give him whatever he asks, whatever it takes, whatever the cost.

Second, ask the Holy Spirit to empower you before you need his power.

As we have seen, we are to be "filled" and empowered by the Spirit every day (Ephesians 5:18). We need the strength of Jesus for every moment (Philippians 4:13). Connect with your Source now, for you will need his power later today.

Third, remember the commitment others have made before you need to make your own.

Hebrews 11 tells us of God's faithful women and men and the often horrific price they paid to serve their Lord. The writer told their stories for a reason: "*Therefore*, since we are surrounded by so great a cloud of witnesses, let us also lay aside every weight, and sin which clings so closely, and let us run with endurance the race that is set before us" (Hebrews 12:1, my emphasis). When we see what others have done, we will be encouraged to do what we can do.

Erwin Lutzer writes:

> During the terrible Boxer Rebellion in China at the turn of the previous century (the leaders were so nicknamed because they practiced gymnastics and calisthenics), the "boxers" captured a mission station, then placed a flat cross on the ground. They gave instruction that those who trampled the cross as they came out of the building would be set free; those who walked around the cross, honoring it, would be executed.
>
> The first seven students trampled the cross under their feet and were released. But the eighth student, a young girl, knelt beside the cross and prayed for strength. Then she slowly walked around the cross to face the firing squad. Strengthened by her example, every one of the more than ninety students followed her to death.

If they could die for Jesus, can't we live for him?

Eight: Be hopeful.

When we partner with God, he uses us in ways we cannot begin to imagine or measure. Our responsibility is to be faithful and hopeful.

In 1983, Edward Kennedy received a membership card from the Moral Majority, which was mailed to him by mistake. Senator Kennedy was famous for his liberal leadership of the Democratic Party, so much so that the founder of the Moral Majority, Reverend Jerry Falwell, called him "the most dangerous American today." When the senator received the card, he called the Moral Majority spokesman, Cal Thomas, to ask if it should be returned. Thomas responded: "No, we don't think anyone is beyond redemption."

It is always too soon to give up on God's ability to change human hearts.

Os Guinness asks, "Can the Christian church in the advanced modern world be renewed and restored even now and be sufficiently changed to have a hope of again changing the world through the power of the gospel? Or is all such talk merely whistling in the dark—pointless, naïve, and irresponsible?"

He then responds: "Let there be no wavering in our answer. Such is the truth and power of the gospel that the church can be revived, reformed, and restored to be a renewing power in the world again. There is no question that the good news of Jesus has effected powerful personal and cultural change in the past. There is no question too that it is still doing so in many parts of the world today. By God's grace it will do so again here in the heart of the advanced modern world where the Christian church is presently in sorry disarray."

He is right: the gospel is transforming lives in "many parts of the world today." In *The Next Christendom*, historian Philip Jenkins describes the explosive growth in Christianity in many parts of the world and predicts that Christians "should enjoy a worldwide boom" in the twenty-first century. However, he adds, "The vast majority of believers will be neither white nor European, nor Euro-American." His research indicates that by 2050 "only about one-fifth of the world's three billion Christians will be non-Hispanic Whites."

While the Lord is clearly at work around the world, he has not abandoned us in America.

In *The Myth of the Dying Church*, Glenn T. Stanton explores the best sociological research available today on the subject of religious commitment in America. What he discovered runs directly counter to the cultural narrative that insists Christianity is in steep decline in our nation and world. On the contrary, he documents remarkable good news for the gospel in our day.

Here are some of his findings:

- Church attendance is at an all-time high both in raw numbers and as a percentage of the population.

- The percentage of young adults who regularly attend evangelical and nondenominational churches has roughly doubled between 1972 and the present day.

- The "nones" (those who say they have no religious affiliation) are not new unbelievers but people who were never committed to the faith and now feel free to admit this fact to pollsters.

- The number of Christians living in the world today is larger than it has been at any point in world history.

In the book's foreword, Baylor University scholar Byron Johnson states, "There is indeed a dramatic decline among some American churches, but this severe decline can be found in a distinct group of churches within theologically liberal mainline Protestantism." By contrast, he states that conservative denominations "are not in decline but are alive and well."

Baylor University sociologist Rodney Stark adds that the percentage of Americans who attend a local church (not necessarily weekly) has grown from 17 percent in 1776 to 34 percent in 1850, 51 percent in 1906, and 69 percent today. A Pew study reported that mainline Protestant churches declined by five million adult members between 2007 and 2014, but evangelical churches grew in absolute numbers by about two million during the same time.

No matter what our secularized culture thinks, Jesus is still King of kings and Lord of lords (Revelation 19:16). He is king of the realm, not just the castle. He is king on Monday, not just on Sunday. And one day every knee will bow and every tongue will confess that he is Lord to the glory of God the Father (Philippians 2:10–11).

Here's the question that changes everything: Is Jesus your king?

The hymn database Hymnary.org saw its page views double in 2020 as the pandemic closed many church buildings. The most popular hymn on the database during that time is still the most popular at this writing: "Holy, Holy, Holy! Lord God Almighty!" This 1826 song proclaims:

Holy, holy, holy! Though the darkness hide thee,
though the eye of sinfulness thy glory may not see,
only thou art holy; there is none beside thee
perfect in pow'r, in love, and purity.

Let's sing these triumphant words with our voices and our lives to the glory of God.

About Dr. Jim Denison

DR. JIM DENISON is a cultural scholar, pastor, and author who helps people respond biblically and redemptively to the vital issues of our day. He is also the cofounder and Chief Vision Officer of the Denison Forum, a Dallas-based nonprofit that comments on current issues through a biblical lens. Through *The Daily Article*, his email newsletter and podcast that reaches a global audience, Dr. Denison guides readers to discern today's news—biblically.

He is a widely sought speaker, podcaster, and subject-matter expert about cultural issues from a biblical perspective. Dr. Denison has been a frequent guest on *Equipped with Chris Brooks* (Moody Radio) and the nationally syndicated *Point of View* with Kerby Anderson (360+ radio stations).

His residencies and fellowships include: Resident Scholar for Ethics with Baylor Scott & White Health, Senior Fellow with the 21st Century Wilberforce Initiative, Senior Fellow for Cultural Studies at Dallas Baptist University's Institute for Global Engagement, and Scholar Fellow with CEO Forum.

He is also a cultural consultant for various organizations that seek a Christian worldview on current events.

Prior to launching Denison Forum in 2009, he pastored churches in Texas and Georgia. He holds a Ph.D. and a Master of Divinity from Southwestern Baptist Theological Seminary. Jim and his wife, Janet, live in Dallas, Texas. They have two sons and four grandchildren.

About Denison Ministries

DENISON MINISTRIES exists to create culture-changing Christians who are committed to advancing the kingdom through that sphere of influence.

We aspire to influence three million Christians every day to experience God through a daily devotional resource (First15.org), to speak into real life through daily cultural commentary (DenisonForum.org), and to bring Jesus into parenting moments (ChristianParenting.org).

Learn more at DenisonMinistries.org.

Acknowledgments

Madeleine L'Engle noted, "You have to write the book that wants to be written."

This book actually *demanded* to be written—the unprecedented crises of our day and the unprecedented opportunities they represent made this project both a burden and a privilege.

By God's grace, my ministry team has helped lift the former and embrace the latter.

Blake Atwood is the Brand Manager for Denison Forum and the editor and manager for this project. His partnership with me extended far beyond copyediting to brainstorming and word crafting. This work is immeasurably better because of his brilliance.

Chris Elkins serves as my chief of staff and makes everything I do more effective and enjoyable.

Katharine Elkins is our outstanding administrative coordinator without whom calendars crash and efficiency fails.

And Steve Yount and Mark Legg are excellent writers and researchers on the Denison Forum team.

Our Denison Ministries Executive Leadership Team directs our ministry's missional growth with such excellence that I am able to focus much of my work on this and related projects.

And our board of directors and financial partners make possible everything we do.

It is a privilege beyond words to share this ministry with my family. Our son Ryan Denison is a brilliant scholar, coauthor of several books with me, author of more than four hundred articles on our website, and daily thought partner. Our son Craig Denison is CEO of Denison Ministries and author and founder of our devotional resource, *First15* (First15.org). His catalytic leadership has grown our audience from 800,000 to more than 6.5 million.

As with every word I have written, church I have pastored, sermon I have preached, and seminary class I have taught, my greatest ministry partner is my wife, Janet. She is a brilliant and anointed Bible teacher (I encourage you to find her resources at foundationswithjanet.org) and the godliest person I have ever known. Her partnership in the gospel and steadfast love are grace gifts to me every day.

Soli Deo gloria.

—*Dr. Jim Denison*

Notes

Foreword: Warning signs

1   **footage of dual natural disasters:** "Rare Video: Japan Tsunami | National Geographic," *National Geographic*, June 13, 2011, https://www.youtube.com/watch?v=oWzdgBNfhQU.

1   **an earthquake struck forty-five miles northeast of Japan:** Becky Oskin, "Japan Earthquake & Tsunami of 2011: Facts and Information," LiveScience.com, September 13, 2017, https://www.livescience.com/39110-japan-2011-earthquake-tsunami-facts.html.

3   **the throes of a culture war:** See, for instance, Jennifer Graham, "The culture war will continue to rage in 2021," *Deseret News*, January 3, 2021, https://www.deseret.com/indepth/2021/1/3/22159761/cancel-culture-wars-abortion-media-partisan-divide-morality-trust-american-community.

3   **how Americans have changed their minds on the moral acceptability:** Cited by Star Parker, "Will Republicans Step Up to Challenge on Values?," *The Daily Signal*, June 16, 2021, https://www.dailysignal.com/2021/06/16/will-republicans-step-up-to-challenge-on-values-lgbtq.

3   **religious beliefs conflict with mainstream American culture:** "White Evangelicals See Trump as Fighting for Their Beliefs, Though Many Have Mixed Feelings About His Personal Conduct," Pew Research Center, March 12, 2020, https://www.pewforum.org/2020/03/12/white-evangelicals-see-trump-as-fighting-for-their-beliefs-though-many-have-mixed-feelings-about-his-personal-conduct/.

3   **white evangelicals expect to lose influence:** Michael Lipka, "Americans far more likely to say evangelicals will lose influence, rather than gain it, under Biden," Pew Research Center, February 10, 2021, https://www.pewresearch.org/fact-tank/2021/02/10/americans-far-more-likely-to-say-evangelicals-will-lose-influence-rather-than-gain-it-under-biden/.

3   **Tsunamis are produced when:** "What is a tsunami?" National Ocean Service, https://oceanservice.noaa.gov/facts/tsunami.html.

4   **those who espouse a specific set of beliefs:** For an expansive treatment from historical and cultural perspectives, see Thomas S. Kidd, *Who Is An Evangelical? The History of a Movement in Crisis* (New Haven, Connecticut: Yale University Press, 2019).

5   **a summary of evangelical distinctives:** "What is an Evangelical?," National Association of Evangelicals, https://www.nae.org/what-is-an-evangelical/.

5   **"religious belief is a matter of personal opinion":** Jeremy Weber, "Christian, What Do You Believe? Probably a Heresy About Jesus, Says Survey," *Christianity Today*, October 16, 2018, https://www.christianitytoday.com/news/2018/october/what-do-christians-believe-ligonier-state-theology-heresy.html.

5   **would make abortion illegal except:** Elana Schor and Emily Swanson, "Poll: White evangelicals distinct on abortion, LGBT policy," Associated Press, January 2, 2020, https://apnews.com/article/donald-trump-us-news-ap-top-news-elections-immigration-8d3eb99934accc2ad795aca0183290a7.

6   **support same-sex marriage:** Tegna, "70% of Americans support same-sex marriage, new national poll shows," WTSP, October 22, 2020, https://www.wtsp.com/article/news/nation-world/same-sex-marriages-majority-support-poll/507-67cdf53a-5175-4211-8850-2c82883a53cc.

7   **"There are times when history and human decisions appear":** Os Guinness, *The American Hour: A Time of Reckoning and the Once and Future Role of Faith* (New York: The Free Press, 1993), 1.

Part 1: Four earthquakes

14   **"a horrible precipice":** Josephus, *Wars of the Jews* 1.21.3.

Chapter 1: The rise of a "post-truth" culture

18   **"cultural current" as "a dominant idea":** Erwin W. Lutzer, *When A Nation Forgets God: 7 Lessons We Must Learn from Nazi Germany* (Chicago, Illinois: Moody Publishers, 2010), 80.

20   **"opinion which is fated":** Charles Sanders Peirce, "How To Make Our Ideas Clear," *Popular Science Monthly*, January 1878, 286–302

21   **"When power is enjoyed without responsibility"**: Hadas Gold, "Meghan and Harry tell four British tabloids they can expect 'zero engagement,'" CNN Business, April 20, 2020, https://www.cnn.com/2020/04/20/media/meghan-harry-tabloids-uk/index.html.

21   **US hospitals came in first:** Justin McCarthy, "Coronavirus Response: Hospitals Rated Best, News Media Worst," Gallup, March 25, 2020, https://news.gallup.com/poll/300680/coronavirus-response-hospitals-rated-best-news-media-worst.aspx.

21   **Americans who said they trust the media:** Art Swift, "Americans' Trust in Mass Media Sinks to New Low," Gallup, September 14, 2016, https://news.gallup.com/poll/195542/americans-trust-mass-media-sinks-new-low.aspx.

21   **"time for journalists to acknowledge":** Michael Schudson, "The Fall, Rise, and Fall of Media Trust," *Columbia Journalism Review*, Winter 2019, https://www.cjr.org/special_report/the-fall-rise-and-fall-of-media-trust.php.

22   **"difficult to discuss belief in God in our society":** Mary Jo Sharp, *Living in Truth: Confident Conversation in a Conflicted Culture* (Nashville, Tennessee: Lifeway Press, 2015), 12.

Chapter 2: The rise of the sexual revolution

25   **"no matter who you are":** "Kellogg Company's Latest Collaboration with GLAAD Unwraps Why 'Boxes Are for Cereal, Not For People'," Kellogg's, last modified May 20, 2021, https://newsroom.kelloggcompany.com/2021-05-20-Kellogg-Companys-Latest-Collaboration-with-GLAAD-Unwraps-Why-Boxes-Are-for-Cereal,-Not-For-People.

25   **Rugrats has been relaunched:** Ryan Foley, "'Rugrats' reboot to feature Betty as lesbian single mom, will be more 'liberally intended show'," *Christian Post*, last modified May 29, 2021, https://www.christianpost.com/news/rugrats-reboot-to-feature-betty-as-lesbian-single-mom.html.

26   **"Love is love is love you see":** David Artavia, "'Blue's Clues' rings in Pride month in new sing-along, starring drag queen Nina West, celebrating LGBTQ families," *Yahoo!*, last modified June 1, 2021, https://www.yahoo.com/entertainment/blues-clues-rings-pride-month-drag-queen-nina-west-lgbtq-families-174301686.html.

26   **first Major League Baseball team to wear Pride uniforms:** April Siese, "San Francisco Giants to be first MLB team to play in Pride uniforms," CBS News, last modified June 2, 2021, https://www. cbsnews.com/news/san-francisco-giants-pride-uniforms-mlb/

26   **Carl Trueman explains our cultural march to sexual "freedom":** Carl Trueman, *The Rise and Triumph of the Modern Self: Cultural Amnesia, Expressive Individualism, and the Road to Sexual Revolution* (Wheaton, Illinois: Crossway, 2020).

27   **"the impact of Wilhelm Reich's thinking":** Jeffrey Escoffier, "The Sexual Revolution, 1960–1980," glbtq, http://www.glbtqarchive.com/ ssh/sexual_revolution_S.pdf.

28   **nineteen million American women:** "Changing Roles for Women," Lumen: Boundless US History, https://courses.lumenlearning.com/ boundless-ushistory/chapter/social-effects-of-the-war/.

29   **"deprave and corrupt those whose minds":** John Philip Jenkins, "Obscenity: Obscenity laws in the 18th and 19th centuries," Britannica, https://www.britannica.com/topic/obscenity#ref34469.

30   **GLAAD has been pressuring television producers:** Megan Townsend, "GLAAD's 'Where We Are on TV' report shows TV is telling more LGBTQ stories than ever," glaad, November 7, 2019, https://www.glaad.org/blog/glaads-where-we-are-tv-report-shows-tv-telling-more-lgbtq-stories-ever.

30   **LGBTQ population of the US was 5.6 percent:** Jeffrey M. Jones, "LGBT Identification Rises to 5.6% in Latest U.S. Estimate," Gallup, last modified February 24, 2021, https://news.gallup.com/ poll/329708/lgbt-identification-rises-latest-estimate.aspx.

31   **Jesus as transgender:** Jim Denison, "Play depicts Jesus as transgender: Four temptations and an amazing story of courage and faith," Denison Forum, June 8, 2021, https://www.denisonforum. org/columns/daily-article/play-depicts-jesus-as-transgender-four-temptations-and-an-amazing-story-of-courage-and-faith/.

31   **legalize prostitution:** Jim Denison, "Should prostitution be legalized? Using secular truth to advance spiritual truth," Denison Forum, June 11, 2021, https://www.denisonforum.org/columns/ daily-article/should-prostitution-be-legalized-using-secular-truth-to-advance-spiritual-truth/.

31   **Advocates for polygamy and polyamory:** See Jim Denison, "Massachusetts city legalizes polyamory: J. I. Packer and the

privilege of standing for biblical truth," Denison Forum, July 21, 2020, https://www.denisonforum.org/columns/daily-article/massachusetts-city-legalizes-polyamory-j-i-packer-and-the-privilege-of-standing-for-biblical-truth/.

32 **incestuous marriage:** For example, see Kathianne Boniello, "New York parent seeks OK to marry their own adult child," *New York Post*, April 10, 2021, https://nypost.com/2021/04/10/new-york-parent-seeks-ok-to-marry-their-own-adult-child/.

32 **sexual relationships between people and animals:** For example, see Jim Denison, "A subject I never expected to address," Denison Forum, April 18, 2016, https://www.denisonforum.org/columns/morality/a-subject-i-never-expected-to-address/.

32 **"When men choose not to believe in God":** Emile Cammaerts, *The Laughing Prophet: The Seven Virtues and G.K. Chesterton*, https://www.goodreads.com/work/quotes/4952463-the-laughing-prophet-the-seven-virtues-and-g-k-chesterton.

Chapter 3: The rise of Critical Theory

33 **thousand-dollar gift given in support of Shannon Braun's campaign:** "Anna Caplan, Chip and Joanna Gaines of 'Fixer Upper' have a relative running for Grapevine-Colleyville ISD school board," *Dallas Morning News*, last modified May 19, 2021, https://www.dallasnews.com/news/elections/2021/05/19/chip-and-joanna-gaines-of-fixer-upper-have-a-relative-running-for-grapevine-colleyville-isd-school-board/.

34 **"Criticism . . . the application of principles":** Robert M. Seiler, "Human Communication in the Critical Theory Tradition," University of Calgary, https://people.ucalgary.ca/~rseiler/critical.html.

34 **"Critical Theory . . . a school of thought that stresses":** Olli-Pekka Moisio, "Critical Theory," *Encyclopedia of Sciences and Religion*, https://link.springer.com/referenceworkentry/10.1007%2F978-1-4020-8265-8_1642.

35 **Cameron Hilditch's overview in *National Review*:** Cameron Hilditch, "How Critical Race Theory Works," *National Review*, May 8, 2021, https://www.nationalreview.com/2021/05/how-critical-race-theory-works.

36 **Bruce Ashford's excellent article in *Public Discourse*:** Bruce Ashford, "Critical Race Theory: Plundering the Egyptians or Worshiping Ba'al?" *Public Discourse: The Journal of the*

Witherspoon Institute, June 6, 2021, https://www.thepublicdiscourse. com/2021/06/76185/. For another excellent overview, see Jonathan Butcher and Mike Gonzalez, "Critical Race Theory, the New Intolerance, and Its Grip on America," The Heritage Foundation, December 7, 2020, https://www.heritage.org/civil-rights/report/ critical-race-theory-the-new-intolerance-and-its-grip-america. For primary documents, see *Critical Race Theory: The Key Writings that Formed the Movement*, ed. Kimberlé Crenshaw, Neil Gotanda, Gary Peller, and Kendall Thomas (New York: The New Press, 1995). For a widely used text, see Richard Delgado and Jean Stefanic, *Critical Race Theory: An Introduction*, 2nd ed. (New York: New York University Press, 2012).

39   **"class" is "rooted in social relations of production":** Cliff Slaughter, *Marxism & the Class Struggle*, https://www.marxists.org/reference/ subject/philosophy/works/en/slaughte.html.

39   **no formal affiliation with a specific Christian denomination:** Aleksandra Sandstrom, "Biden is only the second Catholic president, but nearly all have been Christians," Pew Research Center, January 20, 2021, https://www.pewresearch.org/fact-tank/2021/01/20/biden-only-second catholic-president-but-nearly-all-have-been-christians-2/.

40   **two-thirds of evangelical Christians are white:** Sarah Eekhoff Zylstra, "1 in 3 American Evangelicals Is a Person of Color," *Christianity Today*, September 6, 2017, https://www.christianitytoday. com/news/2017/september/1-in-3-american-evangelicals-person-of-color-prri-atlas.html.

40   **"We tend to talk about race inequality":** Quoted by Katy Steinmetz, "She Coined the Term 'Intersectionality' Over 30 Years Ago. Here's What It Means to Her Today," *TIME*, February 20, 2020, https://time. com/5786710/kimberle-crenshaw-intersectionality/.

41   **"The accusations that get thrown at you":** Mikey O'Connell, "Chip and Joanna Gaines on Walking Away From 'Fixer Upper,' Launching Magnolia Network and the Criticism That Stings the Most," *The Hollywood Reporter*, last modified June 30, 2021, https://www. hollywoodreporter.com/tv/tv-features/chip-joanna-gaines-fixer-upper-magnolia-network-1234975027/.

Chapter 4: The rise of secular religion

43   **The United Nations Committee on the Rights of the Child:** Laurie Goodstein, Nick Cumming-Bruce, and Jim Yardley, "UN Panel Criticizes the Vatican Over Sexual Abuse," *New York Times*, 5

February 2014, https://www.nytimes.com/2014/02/06/world/europe/un-panel-assails-vatican-over-sex-abuse-by-priests.html.

44   **Richard Dawkins calls religion "the root of all evil"**: Richard Dawkins, "Viruses of the Mind" http://www.biolinguagem.com/ling_cog_cult/dawkins_1991_virusesofthemind.pdf.

44   **"science must destroy religion"**: Sam Harris, "Science must destroy religion," SamHarris.org, January 2, 2006, https://samharris.org/science-must-destroy-religion/.

44   **"The Christian church has long been understood"**: R. Albert Mohler, Jr., *We Cannot Be Silent: Speaking Truth to a Culture Redefining Sex, Marriage, & the Very Meaning of Right & Wrong* (Nashville, Tennessee: Nelson Books, 2015), 3.

44   **Billy Graham . . . "most admired"**: Jeffrey M. Jones, "Obama, Clinton Continue Reign as Most Admired," Gallup, December 30, 2013, https://news.gallup.com/poll/166646/obama-clinton-continue-reign-admired-man-woman.aspx.

45   **"a petty, unjust, unforgiving control-freak"**: Richard Dawkins, *The God Delusion* (Boston, Mass: Houghton Mifflin Company, 2006), 31.

45   **"The secular mind in the past"**: Robert Coles, *The Secular Mind* (Princeton, NJ: Princeton University Press, 1999), 185–6.

46   **when the Christian movement began as the "first culture"**: Stephen McAlpine, *Being the Bad Guys: How to Live for Jesus in a World That Says You Shouldn't* (n.p.: The Good Book Company, 2021), Kindle.

46   **Discriminating against Christians**: This section is adapted from Jim Denison, "Respected to Irrelevant to Dangerous: Does Religion Poison Everything?" (Dallas, Texas: Denison Forum, 2015), https://assets.denisonforum.org/pdf/books/respected-to-irrelevant-to-dangerous-does-religion-poison-everything.pdf.

46   **"the most dramatic religion story"**: John L. Allen, Jr., *The Global War on Christians: Dispatches from the Front Lines of Anti-Christian Persecution* (New York: Image, 2013) 1, 17, 1. For examples, see Jim Denison, "Respected to Irrelevant to Dangerous: Does Religion Poison Everything?" (Dallas, Texas: Denison Forum, 2015), https://assets.denisonforum.org/pdf/books/respected-to-irrelevant-to-dangerous-does-religion-poison-everything.pdf.

47   **"extreme conservatives"**: Leonardo Blair, "Some Conservatives 'Have No Place in the State of New York,' Declares NY Gov. Andrew

Cuomo; Sean Hannity Says He Will Leave and Take His Money With Him," *The Christian Post*, January 21, 2014, https://www. christianpost.com/news/some-conservatives-have-no-place-in-the-state-of-new-york-declares-n-y-gov-andrew-cuomo-sean-hannity-says-he-will-leave-and-take-his-money-with-him-113079/.

47   **"absolutely right"**: Leonardo Blair, "NYC Mayor Bill de Blasio Agrees with Gov. Cuomo; 'Extreme' Conservatives Not Welcome in NY State," *The Christian Post*, January 24, 2014, https://www. christianpost.com/news/nyc-mayor-bill-de-blasio-agrees-with-gov-cuomo-extreme-conservatives-not-welcome-in-ny-state-113330/.

47   **"more courage for someone like Chris Broussard"**: John Blake, "When Christians become a 'hated minority,'" CNN, May 5, 2013, https://religion.blogs.cnn.com/2013/05/05/when-christians-become-a-hated-minority/.

47   **"They just do not want to bring up that they are religious"**: Barbara Bradley Hagerty, "Christian Academics Cite Hostility On Campus," NPR, August 3, 2010, https://www.npr.org/templates/story/story.php?storyId=128959747.

47   **called evangelical Christians "religious extremists"**: Nicole Menzie, "Evangelical Christianity, Catholicism Labeled 'Extremist' in Army Presentation," *The Christian Post*, April 6, 2013, https://www. christianpost.com/news/evangelical-christianity-catholicism-labeled-extremist-in-army-presentation-93353/.

48   **A fourteen-year-old honors student:** Todd Starnes, "Texas School Punishes Boy for Opposing Homosexuality," Fox News, September 22, 2011, https://www.foxnews.com/us/texas-school-punishes-boy-for-opposing-homosexuality.

48   **A nineteen-year-old student:** Dave Bohon, "Calif. Univ. Officials Apologize After Student Told to Remove Cross Necklace," *The New American*, July 4, 2013, https://thenewamerican.com/calif-univ-officials-apologize-after-student-told-to-remove-cross-necklace/.

48   **examples of rising discrimination against Christians:** "Christian victims of rising 'hostility' from gov't and secular groups, report says," Fox News, August 26, 2012, https://www.foxnews.com/us/christians-victims-of-rising-hostility-from-govt-and-secular-groups-report-says.

48   **"small act of vengeance"**: Ben Johnson, "'Angry Queers': Christians are 'scum,' deserve 'hammers through their windows,'" LifeSiteNews, April 27, 2012, https://www.lifesitenews.com/news/angry-queers-christians-are-scum-deserve-hammers-through-their-windows/.

49   **"If this event is not shut down":** Brittany Smith, "Christian Hate Crime in Illinois: School Attacked for 'Homophobic' Guest," *The Christian Post*, October 17, 2011, https://www.christianpost.com/news/christian-hate-crime-in-illinois-school-attacked-for-homophobic-guests-58356/.

49   **218 hate crimes against Christians in 2019:** "United States of America," OSCE ODIHR Hate Crime Reporting, https://hatecrime.osce.org/united-states-america.

49   **"Desecration of Catholic Churches":** Francis X. Rocca, "Desecration of Catholic Churches Across US Leaves Congregations Shaken," *The Wall Street Journal*, July 22, 2020, https://www.wsj.com/articles/desecration-of-catholic-churches-across-u-s-leaves-congregations-shaken-11595451973.

49   **the *Tennessee Tribune* reported on recent crimes:** "Churches vandalized across the US," *The Tennessee Tribune*, July 24, 2020, https://tntribune.com/churches-vandalized-across-the-us/.

50   **Twitter locked the magazine out of its account:** Brandon Showalter, "Twitter suspends Christian magazine for saying Biden's trans nominee is a man, not a woman," *The Christian Post*, January 29, 2021, https://www.christianpost.com/news/twitter-suspends-christian-mag-over-biden-trans-nominee-tweet.html.

51   **"a thinly veiled and pathetic excuse for censorship":** Brandon Showalter, "Facebook bans Christian prof. from platform for opposing Biden's transgender military policy," *The Christian Post*, January 28, 2021, https://www.christianpost.com/news/facebook-bans-christian-prof-opposing-bidens-transgender-policies.html.

51   **"Censorship on Facebook and some other social media":** Tyler O'Neil, "Disagreeing With Biden's Transgender Policy Is 'Incitement' Now? Facebook Says So . . .," PJ Media, January 26, 2021, https://pjmedia.com/news-and-politics/tyler-o-neil/2021/01/26/disagreeing-with-bidens-transgender-policy-is-incitement-now-facebook-says-so-n1411958.

51   **Twitter's rules . . . regarding "hateful conduct":** "Hateful conduct policy," Twitter, https://help.twitter.com/en/rules-and-policies/hateful-conduct-policy.

51   **Facebook similarly defines hate speech:** "Community Standards," Facebook, https://transparency.fb.com/policies/community-standards/hate-speech/.

52   **Why religion is considered dangerous:** This section is also adapted from "Respected to Irrelevant to Dangerous."

53   **"an age of increasingly aggressive nationalism":** Keith Ward, *Is Religion Dangerous?* (Grand Rapids, Michigan: William B. Eerdmans Publishing Company, 2006), 140–1.

55   **"I don't believe in Heaven and Hell":** Celebatheists.com, https://www.celebatheists.com/wiki/George_Clooney.

Chapter 5: The Equality Act

63   **John Sherwood is the seventy-one-year-old minister:** Emily Wood, "Preacher arrested for preaching biblical marriage from Genesis on a London street," *The Christian Post*, May 4, 2021, https://www.christianpost.com/news/preacher-arrested-for-preaching-biblical-marriage-on-uk-street.html?clickType=link-most-popular.

64   **"It must be emphasized that religions":** "Obergefell et. al. v. Hodges, Director, Ohio Department of Health, et. al." Supreme Court of the United States, October term, 2014, https://www.supremecourt.gov/opinions/14pdf/14-556_3204.pdf, 27.

64   **"the most invasive threat to religious liberty ever proposed in America":** Andrew T. Walker, "The Equality Act Accelerates Anti-Christian Bias," The Gospel Coalition, March 11, 2019, https://www.thegospelcoalition.org/article/equality-act-anti-christian/.

64   **amend the Civil Rights Acts of 1964:** Kenneth Craycraft, "What to Know About the Equality Act," *First Things*, https://www.firstthings.com/web-exclusives/2021/01/what-to-know-about-the-equality-act.

65   **Here's what this means in practice:** For more, see "Heritage Explains the Equality Act," The Heritage Foundation, https://www.heritage.org/gender/heritage-explains/the-equality-act.

65   **"The Equality Act would become the first major piece of legislation":** David S. Dockery, "The Equality Act, People of Faith, and Religious Freedom," International Alliance for Christian Education (IACE), April 18, 2021, https://iace.education/blog/ca9jf136het68kb7e92mrsc48bo1qr.

66   **"threatens religious colleges and universities":** Sarah Kramer, "Think the 'Equality Act' Will Spare Churches and Religious Schools? Think Again," Alliance Defending Freedom, March 4, 2021, https://

www.adfchurchalliance.org/post/think-the-equality-act-will-spare-churches-and-religious-schools-think-again.

66   **Seven out of every ten students who come to a Christian college:** Morgan Lee, "The Equality Act Through the Eyes of a Christian College President," *Christianity Today*, March 18, 2021, https://www.christianitytoday.com/ct/podcasts/quick-to-listen/equality-act-lgbtq-religious-liberty-houghton-podcast.html.

66   **jeopardize Christian colleges' ability to maintain their stated mission:** Lee.

66   **Title VII of the 1964 Civil Rights Act:** "Title VII of the Civil Rights Act of 1964," US Equal Employment Opportunity Commission, https://www.eeoc.gov/statutes/title-vii-civil-rights-act-1964.

66   **this prohibition extends to sexual orientation and gender identity:** "Bostock v. Clayton County, Georgia," SupremeCourt.gov, https://www.supremecourt.gov/opinions/19pdf/17-1618_hfci.pdf.

67   **the Equality Act would codify *Bostock*:** "How the Equality Act Could Affect Churches and Religious Organizations," Church Law Center of California, April 20, 2021, https://www.churchlawcenter.com/church-law/how-the-equality-act-could-affect-churches-and-religious-organizations/.

67   **"The Equality Act expands the meaning of public accommodations":** David S. Dockery, "The Equality Act, People of Faith, and Religious Freedom," International Alliance for Christian Education (IACE), April 18, 2021, https://iace.education/blog/ca9jf136het68kb7e92mrsc48bo1qr.

67   **a "medical condition" such as abortion could be protected:** Melanie Israel, "Equality Act Is Trojan Horse for Abortion Lobby and More," The Daily Signal, February 22, 2021, https://www.dailysignal.com/2021/02/22/equality-act-is-trojan-horse-for-abortion-lobby-and-more/.

68   **The court cited the RFRA in issuing its ruling:** Nicole Russell, "Federal Court Upholds Conscience Protections for Doctors," The Daily Signal, January 25, 2021, https://www.dailysignal.com/2021/01/25/federal-court-upholds-conscience-protections-for-doctors/.

68   **President Biden has stated that he would sign it:** "The Biden Plan to Advance LGBTQ+ Equality in America and Around the World," BidenHarris, https://joebiden.com/lgbtq-policy/.

69   **blocking posts critical of President Biden's transgender policy:** Brandon Showalter, "Twitter suspends Christian magazine for saying Biden's trans nominee is a man, not a woman," *The Christian Post,* January 29, 2021, https://www.christianpost.com/news/twitter-suspends-christian-mag-over-biden-trans-nominee-tweet.html.

69   **examples of social media . . . restricting Christian viewpoints:** Holly Meyer, "Conservatives to Facebook, Google and Twitter: Stop censoring our posts," *Tennessean,* March 2, 2018, https://www.tennessean.com/story/news/religion/2018/03/01/facebook-google-twitter-christian-evangelical-conservative-social-media-censorship/382244002/.

70   **a chapter-length examination of the transgender debate:** This chapter is available on our website: https://assets.denisonforum.org/pdf/transgender-issue.pdf.

70   **"radical feminist organization . . . This is an emergency":** Virginia Allen, "'This Is an Emergency,' Feminist Says About Future of Women's Sports," The Daily Signal, January 28, 2021, https://www.dailysignal.com/2021/01/28/this-is-an-emergency-feminist-says-about-future-of-womens-sports/.

70   **"end sports programs and scholarships set aside for women and girls":** "House to Vote on the Equality Act: Take Action Now!" WOLF, February 17, 2021, https://www.womensliberationfront.org/news/housetovoteonequalityact.

71   **"'Destroy Our Daughters Act'":** Margot Cleveland, "Why the 'Equality Act' Democrats Want To Pass This Week Should Really Be Called The 'Destroy Our Daughters Act,'" *The Federalist,* February 22, 2021, https://thefederalist.com/2021/02/22/why-the-equality-act-democrats-want-to-pass-this-week-should-really-be-called-the-destroy-our-daughters-act/.

71   **Pastor Esteban Carrasco and House of Destiny Ministries:** Sarah Kramer, "Think the 'Equality Act' Will Spare Churches and Religious Schools? Think Again," Alliance Defending Freedom, March 4, 2021, https://www.adfchurchalliance.org/post/think-the-equality-act-will-spare-churches-and-religious-schools-think-again.

71   **transgender Americans constitute only 0.6 percent of our adult population:** Bill Chappell, "1.4 Million Adults Identify As Transgender In America, Study Says," NPR, June 30, 2016, https://www.npr.org/sections/thetwo-way/2016/06/30/484253324/1-4-million-adults-identify-as-transgender-in-america-study-says.

72   **"The menace to religious freedom"**: Os Guinness, *The Global Public Square: Religious Freedom and the Making of a World Safe for Diversity* (Downers Grove, Illinois: IVP Books, 2013), 17.

Chapter 6: Beyond the Equality Act

76   **"If they're going to politically weaponize religion"**: Reported by Anugrah Kumar, "Democrat warns Catholic Church it may be stripped of tax-exempt status if politicians denied communion," *The Christian Post*, June 21, 2021https://www.christianpost.com/news/democrats-warn-catholic-church-against-denying-them-communion.html.

76   **"no national policy on withholding Communion from politicians"**: Michelle Boorstein, "After controversy, U.S. Catholic bishops say there will be 'no national policy on withholding Communion from politicians'," *New York Times*, last modified June 25, 2021, https://www.washingtonpost.com/religion/2021/06/25/catholic-bishops-communion-biden-abortion/.

76   **Christians Engaged applied for 501(c)(3) nonprofit status with the Internal Revenue Service:** "Christians Engaged," First Liberty, https://firstliberty.org/cases/christians-engaged/.

77   **"You instruct individuals on issues that are prominent in political campaigns"**: "Christians Engaged," Department of the Treasury, Internal Revenue Service, May 18, 2021, https://firstliberty.org/wp-content/uploads/2021/06/Christians-Engaged-IRS-Determination-Letter_Redacted.pdf.

77   **"the abuses that thousands of LGBTQ+ students endured at taxpayer-funded religious colleges"**: William Trollinger and Susal L. Trollinger, "What a Title IX lawsuit might mean for religious universities," *The Conversation*, June 15, 2021, https://theconversation.com/what-a-title-ix-lawsuit-might-mean-for-religious-universities-159411.

78   **"The reality is each case has to be investigated individually"**: Katie Rogers, "Title IX Protections Extend to Transgender Students, Educatio Dept. Says," *The New York Times*, June 16, 2021, https://www.nytimes.com/2021/06/16/us/politics/title-ix-transgender-students.html.

79   **"deeply bigoted anti-LGBTQ+ policies"**: Hemal Jhaveri, "Oral Roberts University isn't the feel good March Madness story we need," *USA Today*, March 23, 2021, https://ftw.usatoday.com/2021/03/oral-roberts-ncaa-anti-lgbtq-code-of-conduct.

See also Jim Denison, "Responding to the Oral Roberts University controversy: Two interrelated imperatives all Christians should embrace today," Denison Forum, March 29, 2021, https://www.denisonforum.org/columns/daily-article/responding-to-the-oral-roberts-university-controversy-two-interrelated-imperatives-all-christians-should-embrace-today/.

79 **"Don't use Dallas Cowboys' name":** Mike Freeman, "Opinion: Don't use Dallas Cowboys' name, AT&T Stadium to mainstream anti-trans hate," *USA Today*, May 5, 2021, https://www.usatoday.com/story/sports/columnist/mike-freeman/2021/05/05/dallas-cowboys-name-att-dont-use-mainstream-anti-trans-hate/4853968001/.

79 **Promise Keepers . . . "focused on helping men live with integrity":** "About Us," Promise Keepers: Men of Integrity, https://promisekeepers.org/promise-keepers/about-us-2/.

79 **Catholic priests in Germany . . . blessing gay unions:** Kirsten, Grieshaber, "German Catholics to bless gay unions despite Vatican ban," Associated Press, May 10, 2021, https://apnews.com/article/europe-lifestyle-religion-f94e1e634f3b80e209d82ce29927deab.

79 **A Baptist church in Indiana ordained a transgender pastor:** Michael Gryboski, "Baptist church ordains first known transgender pastor in denomination's history," *The Christian Post*, June 16, 2021, https://www.christianpost.com/church-ministries/cbf-church-ordains-first-known-transgender-pastor-in-its-history.html.

79 **A Methodist church in Illinois confirmed for ordination a gay man who is also a drag queen:** Jim Denison, "Church confirms drag queen for ordination: The urgency and power of personal morality," Denison Forum, May 3, 2021, https://www.denisonforum.org/columns/daily-article/church-confirms-drag-queen-for-ordination-the-urgency-and-power-of-personal-morality/.

80 **58 percent of white evangelicals and 70 percent of black Protestants believe cohabiting is acceptable:** David J. Ayers, "The Cohabitation Dilemma Comes for America's Pastors," *Christianity Today*, March 16, 2021, https://www.christianitytoday.com/ct/2021/april/cohabitation-dilemma-comes-for-american-pastors-ayers.html.

80 **half of US Christians said casual sex between consenting adults is sometimes or always acceptable:** Jeff Diamant, "Half of US Christians say casual sex between consenting adults is sometimes or always acceptable," Pew Research Center, August 31, 2020, https://www.pewresearch.org/fact-tank/2020/08/31/half-of-u-s-christians-say-casual-sex-between-consenting-adults-is-sometimes-or-always-acceptable/.

80   **"The Bible clearly considers homosexuality a sin"**: Walter Wink, "Biblical Perspectives on Homosexuality," https://reconcilingworks. org/images/stories/downloads/resources/003_Homosexuality_and_ the_Bible-Wink.pdf.

81   **claim that the biblical era knew nothing of same-sex orientation:** Matthew Vines, *God and the Gay Christian: The Biblical Case in Support of Same-Sex Relationships* (New York: Convergent Books, 2014); David P. Gushee, *Changing Our Mind* (Canton, MI: David Crumm Media, 2014).

81   **"Verily there is that which is more contrary to Christianity"**: Quoted by Os Guinness, *Renaissance: The Power of the Gospel However Dark the Times* (Downers Grove, Illinois: IVP Books, 2014), 7.

Chapter 7: "Woke" business

83   **More than four hundred companies have signed on to support the Equality Act:** Dee-Ann Durbin, "More than 400 businesses back LGBTQ rights act," ABC News, April 27, 2021, https://abcnews. go.com/Politics/wireStory/400-businesses-back-lgbtq-rights- act-77341660.

83   **Burger King . . . donation to the Human Rights Campaign:** @ BurgerKing, Twitter, June 3, 2021, https://twitter.com/BurgerKing/ status/1400618810571362305?s=20.

83   **"unacceptable" and a "step backwards":** "Coca-Cola CEO calls Georgia voting law 'unacceptable' and a 'step backwards,'" CNBC, March 31, 2021, (https://www.cnbc.com/video/2021/03/31/coca-cola- ceo-says-georgia-voting-law-a-step-backwards.html.

83   **voted to remove Coca-Cola machines:** Alyssa Newcomb, "North Carolina county bans Coca-Cola machines after company criticizes Georgia voting law," *Yahoo!* June 4, 2021, https://www.yahoo.com/ news/north-carolina-county-bans-coca-115733880.html.

84   **"a clear nod to all the fabulous drag queens":** Jim Denison, "LEGO drag queen figures and a hit piece on Chip and Joanna Gaines: Learning an important lesson from our fallen culture," Denison Forum, May 27, 2021, https://www.denisonforum.org/columns/ daily-article/lego-drag-queen-figures-and-a-hit-piece-on-chip-and- joanna-gaines-learning-an-important-lesson-from-our-fallen-culture/.

84   **voluntary private markets are more productive than government-run economies:** For more, see Christina Majaski, "Invisible Hand Definition," Investopedia, July 23, 2020, https://www.investopedia.com/terms/i/invisiblehand.asp.

84   **"The business of business is business":** Nick O'Donohoe, "What is the true business of business?," *World Economic Forum*, last modified February 25, 2016, https://www.weforum.org/agenda/2016/02/the-business-of-business-is-what/.

85   **workplace culture behind only work-life balance:** Emma Featherstone, "For young job seekers, a potential workplace needs to be woke," *The Guardian*, July 9, 2019, https://www.theguardian.com/careers/2019/jul/09/for-young-job-seekers-a-potential-workplace-needs-to-be-woke.

85   **a diverse workforce was important:** Jennifer Miller, "For younger job seekers, diversity and inclusion in the workplace aren't a preference. They're a requirement," *Washington Post*, February 18, 2021, https://www.washingtonpost.com/business/2021/02/18/millennial-genz-workplace-diversity-equity-inclusion/.

86   **Yuval Levin diagnoses the conflicts, rancor, and despair of our present culture:** Yuval Levin, *A Time to Build: From Family and Community to Congress and the Campus, How Recommitting to Our Institutions Can Revive the American Dream* (New York: Basic Books, 2020).

87   **"introducing women into combat":** Lieutenant Neil L. Golightly, USN, "No Right to Fight," US Naval Institute, December 1987, https://www.usni.org/magazines/proceedings/1987/december/no-right-fight.

87   **"painful because it is wrong":** Jenny Gross, "Boeing Communications Chief Resigns over 33-Year-Old Article," *The New York Times*, July 8, 2020, https://www.nytimes.com/2020/07/08/business/boeing-resignation-niel-golightly.html.

87   **"Cancel culture . . . removing of support for public figures":** "What It Means to Get 'Canceled," Merriam-Webster, https://www.merriam-webster.com/words-at-play/cancel-culture-words-were-watching.

87   **Goya Foods CEO Bob Unanue appeared at a press conference with President Donald Trump:** Jim Denison, "CEO faces boycott for appearing with President Trump: Explaining and responding to 'cancel culture,'" Denison Forum, July 16, 2020, https://www.denisonforum.org/columns/daily-article/ceo-faces-boycott-for-appearing-with-president-trump-explaining-and-responding-to-cancel-culture/.

88   **5.6 percent of Americans identify as LGBTQ:** Jeffrey M. Jones, "LGBT Identification Rises to 5.6% in Latest US Estimate," Gallup, February 24, 2021, https://news.gallup.com/poll/329708/lgbt-identification-rises-latest-estimate.aspx.

88   **nearly 70 percent support nondiscrimination protections for LGBTQ persons:** Tim Fitzsimons, "Majority of Americans back LGBTQ protections—but support is sliding," *NBC News*, March 26, 2019, https://www.nbcnews.com/feature/nbc-out/majority-americans-back-lgbtq-protections-support-sliding-n987156.

88   **"On behalf of Apple, I'm standing up to oppose this new wave of legislation":** Tim Cook, "Tim Cook: Pro-discrimination 'religious freedom' laws are dangerous," *The Washington Post*, March 29, 2015, https://www.washingtonpost.com/opinions/pro-discrimination-religious-freedom-laws-are-dangerous-to-america/2015/03/29/bdb4ce9e-d66d-11e4-ba28-f2a685dc7f89_story.html.

89   **algorithms that amplify "woke" voices:** Annelise Butler, "Why Big Tech Companies Continue to Lose Public's Trust," *The Daily Signal*, May 6, 2021, https://www.dailysignal.com/2021/05/06/why-big-tech-companies-continue-to-lose-publics-trust/.

90   **consumer spending comprises 70 percent of the US economy:** Kimberly Amadeo, "Components of GDP Explained," the balance, June 26, 2020, https://www.thebalance.com/components-of-gdp-explanation-formula-and-chart-3306015.

90   **the US is the largest advertising market in the world:** "Advertising spending in North America from 2000 to 2022," statista, https://www.statista.com/statistics/429036/advertising-expenditure-in-north-america/.

90   **Brendan Eich was CEO of Mozilla:** Susan Adams, "Mozilla's Brendan Eich: Persecutor Or Persecuted," *Forbes*, April 4, 2014, https://www.forbes.com/sites/susanadams/2014/04/04/mozillas-brendan-eich-persecutor-or-persecuted/?sh=318de77a35cd.

90   **A Christian in New Jersey filed a wrongful termination suit against Starbucks:** Jesse T. Jackson, "Christian Starbucks Employee Fired for Refusing to Wear Company 'Pride' Shirt," ChurchLeaders, November 30, 2020, https://churchleaders.com/news/386028-christian-starbucks-employee-fired-for-refusing-to-wear-company-pride-shirt.html.

91   **A Christian physician assistant was fired in 2020:** Marlee Tomlinson, "First Liberty Fights on Behalf of Physician Assistant Fired Due to His Religious Beliefs," First Liberty, November 13, 2020, https://firstliberty.org/news/physicians-assistant-fired/.

91 **chief economist for a financial firm:** Jerry Bowyer, "Companies censor shareholder questions about anti-religious liberty law at annual meetings," *The Christian Post*, May 3, 2021, https://www.christianpost.com/news/companies-censor-questions-about-anti-religious-liberty-law.html.

91 **evangelical Protestants comprise 25.4 percent of the American population:** "Religious Landscape Study," Pew Research Center, Centerhttps://www.pewforum.org/religious-landscape-study/.

91 **42 percent of evangelical Protestants earn more than $50,000 a year:** "Religious Landscape Study: Income distribution," Pew Research Center, https://www.pewforum.org/religious-landscape-study/income-distribution/.

92 **"To combine business with religion":** John Caird, *Religion in Common Life* (Philadelphia, PA: Henry Longstreth, 1856; reprinted by Kessinger Legacy Reprints), 1.

Chapter 8: Designer babies and chimeras

93 **"Do adults with capacity hold the ultimate authority over their own bodies":** Alexis Drutchas, "In America, is bodily autonomy a human right?" CNN, June 3, 2021, https://www.cnn.com/2021/06/03/opinions/bodily-autonomy-abortion-access-transgender-health-paxton-smith-drutchas/index.html.

95 **"pregnancy, childbirth, or a related medical condition":** "HR 5–Equality Act," Congress.gov, https://www.congress.gov/bill/117th-congress/house-bill/5/text.

95 **"This outrageous so-called 'Equality Act'":** "'Equality Act' Makes Abortion a Federal Right," Liberty Counsel, March 4, 2021, https://lc.org/newsroom/details/030421-equality-act-makes-abortion-a-federal-right.

96 **"the greatest revolution since Leonardo":** Francis S. Collins, *The Language of Life: DNA and the Revolution in Personalized Medicine* (New York: HarperCollins, 2010) 5.

98 **one million embryos created by IVF:** National Embryo Donation Center, https://www.embryodonation.org/.

99 **More than one hundred thousand Americans are currently on waiting lists for a donated organ:** "Organ Donor Statistics," organdonor.gov, (https://www.organdonor.gov/learn/organ-donation-statistics.

103 **CRISPR to engineer twin girls:** Dennis Normile, "CRISPR bombshell: Chinese researcher claims to have created gene-edited twins," *Science*, November 26, 2018, https://www.science.org/news/2018/11/crispr-bombshell-chinese-researcher-claims-have-created-gene-edited-twins.

103 **"three-parent babies":** Emily Mullen, "Patient advocates and scientists launch push to lift ban on 'three-parent IVF,'" STAT, April 16. 2019, https://www.statnews.com/2019/04/16/mitochondrial-replacement-three-parent-ivf-ban/.

104 **"chimera" . . . cells with different embryonic origins:** "Human/Non-Human Chimeras," Stanford Encyclopedia of Philosophy, first published May 21, 2009, substantive revision July 21 2014, https://plato.stanford.edu/entries/chimeras/.

104 **combined human stem cells with monkey embryos:** Tao Tan, et. al., "Chimeric contribution of human extended pluripotent stem cells to monkey embryos ex vivo," *Cell*, April 15, 2021, https://www.cell.com/cell/fulltext/S0092-8674(21)00305-6.

105 **"toward ways to ease suffering. . . . I can't stand in judgment":** Quoted by Cathy Lynn Grossman, "California's End of Life Option law: More peaceful death or moral quicksand?" Religion News Service, June 7, 2016, https://religionnews.com/2016/06/07/californias-end-of-life-option-law-more-peaceful-deaths-or-moral-quicksand/.

Chapter 9: Defending biblical truth with reason and relevance

116 **Skepticism arose more than three centuries before Christ:** For more, see "Ancient Greek Skepticism," Internet Encyclopedia of Philosophy, https://iep.utm.edu/skepanci/.

117 **"Just as one cannot deny the principle of non-contradiction":** R. J. Snell, "God and Public Reason," *Public Discourse: The Journal of the Witherspoon Institute*, June 19, 2021, https://www.thepublicdiscourse.com/2021/06/76402/.

118 **You and I are complicit in this attack on Islam:** For more, see Jim Denison, *Radical Islam: What You Need to Know* (Elevation Press, 2011).

121 **excellent archaeological data:** Sources include Jeffrey L. Sheler, *Is the Bible True?* (HarperSanFrancisco, 1999; John Arthur Thompson, *The Bible and Archaeology*, ed. rev. (Grand Rapids, Michigan: Eerdmans, 1982); Merrill F. Unger, *Archaeology and the New Testament* (Grand Rapids, Michigan: Zondervan, 1962).

122   **an inscription . . . dated to the ninth century before Christ:** John Noble Wilford, "From Israeli Site, News of House of David," *The New York Times*, August 6, 1993, https://www.nytimes.com/1993/08/06/world/from-israeli-site-news-of-house-of-david.html.

124   **Jeane Dixon made the news:** Norman Geisler and Ron Brooks, *When Skeptics Ask: A Handbook On Christian Evidences* (Wheaton, Illinois: Victor Books, 1990) 91.

127   *Representative Messianic prophecies:* This discussion follows the treatment by Josh McDowell, *The New Evidence that Demands a Verdict* (Nashville: Thomas Nelson, 1999) 167–94. McDowell's discussion is helpful in that it depends heavily upon Jewish interpretation of the Old Testament sources cited.

Chapter 10: Defending biblical sexuality with grace and truth

136   **"Like most theologically conservative Christians":** Matthew Vines, *God and the Gay Christian: The Biblical Case in Support of Same-Sex Relationships* (New York: Convergent Books, 2014), 2.

137   **its authors deal with each of Vines' proposals in turn:** *God and the Gay Christian? A Response to Matthew Vines*, ed. R. Albert Mohler Jr. (Louisville, Kentucky: SBTS Press, 2014), 22.

138   **"Biblical Christianity can neither endorse same-sex marriage . . . The church has often failed people with same-sex attractions":** Mohler, 23.

139   **"deeply-hurt-by-the-church-but-still-committed-to-Jesus-gay Christians":** David P. Gushee, *Changing Our Mind: A call from America's leading evangelical ethics scholar for full acceptance of LGBT Christians in the Church* (Canton, Michigan: Read The Spirit Books, 2014), 122.

139   **arguments from God's purported design for humans:** Gushee, 94.

141   **"covenantal-marital sexual ethical standard":** Gushee, 106.

141   **three of the sixteen seasons have resulted in marriages:** "The Bachelorette," Wikipedia, last modified July 14, 2021, https://en.wikipedia.org/wiki/The_Bachelorette

141   **"I talk about sex in a very casual way":** Jim Denison, "Why Katie Thurston of 'The Bachelorette' is making headlines: Four biblical steps to living with character God can bless," Denison Forum, June 14, 2021, https://www.denisonforum.org/columns/daily-article/why-

katie-thurston-of-the-bachelorette-is-making-headlines-four-biblical-steps-to-living-with-character-god-can-bless/.

141   **"Being nonjudgmental is at the heart of sex positivity":** Korin Miller, "Katie Thurston wants to talk about sex on 'The Bachelorette.' Here's why experts say it's 'a good move for this franchise,'" *Yahoo!* June 8, 2021, https://www.yahoo.com/lifestyle/bachelorette-katie-thurston-sex-positivity-184220174.html.

143   **Sixty-nine percent of Americans say sex between an unmarried man and woman is morally acceptable:** See Aaron Earls, "American's List of Immoral Actions Keeps Shrinking," Lifeway Research, June 6, 2018, https://lifewayresearch.com/2018/06/06/americans-list-of-immoral-actions-keeps-shrinking/.

143   **the youth suicide rate is the highest it has been:** Emily Seymour, "Gen Z: Studies Show Higher Rates of Depression," VOA, August 25, 2019, https://www.voanews.com/a/student-union_gen-z-studies-show-higher-rates-depression/6174520.html.

143   **percentage of children born out of wedlock:** Stephanie J. Ventura and Christine A. Bachrach, "Nonmarital Childbearing in the United States, 1940–99," National Vital Statistics Reports, October 18, 2000, https://www.cdc.gov/nchs/data/nvsr/nvsr48/nvs48_16.pdf; "Unmarried Childbearing," Centers for Disease Control and Prevention, https://www.cdc.gov/nchs/fastats/unmarried-childbearing.htm.

143   **children in single-parent homes:** George A. Akerlof and Janet L. Yellen, "An analysis of out-of-wedlock births in the United States," Brookings Institution, August 1, 1996, https://www.brookings.edu/research/an-analysis-of-out-of-wedlock-births-in-the-united-states/.

143   **STDs have reached all-time highs for six consecutive years:** Gabriela Miranda, "STDs reach all-time high for sixth consecutive year in the US. Is your state in the top 10?" *USA Today*, June 15, 2021, https://www.yahoo.com/news/stds-reach-time-high-sixth-194953476.html.

143   **86 percent of abortions are obtained by unmarried women:** "Percentage distribution of US women obtaining abortions in nonhospital settings and of all US women aged 15–44, and abortion index, by selected characteristics, 2014 and 2008," Guttmacher.org, https://www.guttmacher.org/sites/default/files/report_downloads/us-abortion-patients-table1.pdf.

143   **The Bible and abortion:** For a larger discussion of this crucial subject, see Jim Denison, *Between Compromise and Courage: The Choice Every Christian Must Make* (Dallas, Texas: Denison Forum, 2021), 31–65.

144   **Abortion is the leading cause of death in America:** Carole Novielli, "Abortion outnumbered each of the top leading causes of death in the US in 2017," Liveaction.org, January 21, 2020, https://www.liveaction.org/news/abortion-outnumbered-leading-causes-death-2017/.

144   **Moral arguments for abortion:** For more on the ethical arguments for and against abortion see Milton A. Gonsalves, *Right & Reason: Ethics in theory and practice*, 9th ed. (Columbus: Merrill Publishing Co., 1989).

146   **such cases typically account for only 1 percent of abortions:** Lawrence B. Finer, Lori F. Frohwirth, Lindsay A. Dauphinee, Susheela Singh and Ann M. Moore, "Reasons U.S. Women Have Abortions: Quantitative and Qualitative Perspectives," Guttmacher Institute, *Perspectives on Sexual and Reproductive Health,* https://www.guttmacher.org/sites/default/files/pdfs/pubs/psrh/full/3711005.pdf.

147   **heroin is so popular:** "DrugFacts: Heroin," National Institute on Drug Abuse, October 2014, https://teens.drugabuse.gov/sites/default/files/drugfacts_heroin_10_14.pdf.

150   **"The embryo has its own autonomy":** Karl Barth, *Church Dogmatics* (Edinburgh: T & T Clark, 1985 [1961]), 3.4.416.

151   **Unprotected intercourse results in pregnancy about 4 percent of the time.:** Virginia Ramey Mollenkott, "Reproductive Choice: Basic to Justice for Women," in *Readings in Christian Ethics*, ed. David K. Clark and Robert V. Rakestraw (Grand Rapids, Michigan: Baker, 1996), 2:27.

152   **a bill that would decriminalize so-called "sex work":** Lincoln Graves, "Proposal would decriminalize prostitution in Oregon," KATU, June 4, 2021, https://katu.com/news/local/proposal-would-decriminalize-prostitution-in-oregon.

152   **"Sex Work is Real Work":** LaLa B. Holston-Zannell, "Sex Work is Real Work, and it's Time to Treat it that Way," ACLU, June 10, 2020, https://www.aclu.org/news/lgbtq-rights/sex-work-is-real-work-and-its-time-to-treat-it-that-way/.

152   **Vice President Kamala Harris:** Terrell Jermaine Starr, "Exclusive: Kamala Harris Calls for Decriminalization of Sex Work, Unequivocally

Calls Trump a Racist and Wants Reparations (Sort of)," *The Root*, February 26, 2019, https://www.theroot.com/exclusive-kamala-harris-calls-for-decriminalization-of-1832883951.

152 **"criminalization of sex work":** Chelsea Cirruzzo, "The Case for Decriminalizing Sex Work," *US News & World Report*, January 11, 2021, https://www.usnews.com/news/health-news/articles/2021-01-11/calls-mount-to-decriminalize-sex-work-in-the-interest-of-public-health.

153 **"prostitution is inherently abusive":** Julie Bindel, "Why prostitution should never be legalized," *The Guardian*, October 11, 2017, https://www.theguardian.com/commentisfree/2017/oct/11/prostitution-legalised-sex-trade-pimps-women.

153 **One study of prostituted women:** Kelly Allen, "Prostitution vs. Human Trafficking: Understanding Exploitation," Exodus Road, March 5, 2021, https://theexodusroad.com/prostitution-vs-human-trafficking-understanding-exploitation/.

153 **"where prostitution is legalized or tolerated":** "The Link Between Prostitution and Sex Trafficking," US Department of State, November 24, 2004, https://2001-2009.state.gov/r/pa/ei/rls/38790.htm.

153 **"countries with legalized prostitution":** "Does Legalizing Prostitution Increase Human Trafficking?" Harvard Law and International Development Society, June 12, 2014, https://orgs.law.harvard.edu/lids/2014/06/12/does-legalized-prostitution-increase-human-trafficking/.

153 **Every day in America:** "Internet Pornography by the Numbers; A Significant Threat to Society," Webroot, https://www.webroot.com/us/en/resources/tips-articles/internet-pornography-by-the-numbers.

154 **when men viewed pictures of sexualized women:** Paul Bloom, "The Ways of Lust," *The New York Times*, November 29, 2013, https://www.nytimes.com/2013/12/01/opinion/sunday/the-ways-of-lust.html.

154 **Pornography . . . . utilizes three basic themes:** Robert Jensen, "Pornography and Sexual Violence," Applied Research Forum: National Online Resource Center on Violence Against Women, https://vawnet.org/material/pornography-and-sexual-violence.

154 **"As pornography has become more acceptable":** Justin Holcomb, "Isn't Porn Harmless?," https://justinholcomb.com/2012/03/05/isnt-porn-harmless/.

154   **"We are now bringing up a generation of boys on cruel, violent porn":** Gail Dines, *Pornland: How Porn Has Hijacked Our Sexuality* (United States: Beacon Press, 2010).

155   **"the prevalence of pornography":** Holcomb.

155   **study of 804 representative Italian teenagers:** "Use of Pornography and Self-Reported Engagement in Sexual Violence Among Adolescents," *European Journal of Developmental Psychology 3* (2006), 265–88.

155   **Men who habitually view pornography:** Nathan Black, "Family Group Releases Study on Effects of Pornography," *The Christian Post*, December 2, 2009, https://www.christianpost.com/news/family-group-releases-study-on-effects-of-pornography-42100/#OEBbUwUw0olkF4GL.99.

155   **exposed to X-rated magazines or videos:** Mary Eberstadt and Mary Anne Layden, *The Social Costs of Pornography: A Statement of Findings and Recommendations* (United States: Witherspoon Institute, 2010).

155   **India banned more than eight hundred pornographic websites:** Nadia Khomami, "India lifts ban on internet pornography after criticism," *The Guardian*, August 5, 2021, "https://www.theguardian.com/culture/2015/aug/05/india-lifts-ban-on-internet-pornography-after-criticisms.

155   **An estimated 293,000 American youths are currently at risk of becoming victims of commercial sexual exploitation:** Amanda Walker-Rodriguez and Rodney Hill, "Human Sex Trafficking," FBI Law Enforcement Bulletin, https://leb.fbi.gov/articles/featured-articles/human-sex-trafficking.

155   **study of arrested child pornography possessors:** Janis Wolak, David Finkelhor, and Kimberly J. Mitchell, "Child-Pornography Possessors Arrested in Internet-Related Crimes: Findings From the National Juvenile Online Victimization Study," National Center for Missing & Exploited Children, http://unh.edu/ccrc/pdf/jvq/CV81.pdf

155   **Child pornography . . . a $20 billion annual industry:** Carl Bialik, "Measuring the Child-Porn Trade," *The Wall Street Journal*, April 18, 2006, https://www.wsj.com/articles/SB114485422875624000.

155   **average age of a trafficked victim:** "Commercial Sexual Exploitation of Children (CSEC) and Child Sexual Abuse (CSA) in the Pacific: A Regional Report," *La Strada International*, https://documentation. lastradainternational.org/doc-center/1295/commercial-sexual-exploitation-of-children-csec-and-child-sexual-abuse-csa-in-the-pacific-a-regional-report.

156   **the slippery slope:** Mary Eberstadt and Mary Anne Layden, *The Social Costs of Pornography: A Statement of Findings and Recommendations* (United States: Witherspoon Institute, 2010).

156   **American Academy of Matrimonial Lawyers:** "Effects of Pornography on Marriage," *Marripedia,* http://marripedia.org/effects_of_pornography_on_marriage.

157   **I highly recommend There's Still Hope:** There's Still Hope: Recovery & Restoration, https://www.theresstillhope.org/.

158   **"How We Got to the Equality Act":** Matthew Lee Anderson, "How We Got to the Equality Act," *Christianity Today*, April 20, 2021, https://www.christianitytoday.com/ct/2021/may-june/lgbt-pride-evangelical-culture-politics-equality-act.html.

Chapter 11: Defending biblical equality with compassion and humility

161   **opposition to the Equality Act:** "US Bishops: Equality Act discriminates against people of faith and threatens unborn life," *Vatican News*, https://www.vaticannews.va/en/church/news/2021-02/bishops-equality-act-usccb-congress-unborn-life.html.

161   **"I do believe that people who want to blatantly discriminate":** "The Equality Act: LGBTQ Rights are Human Rights," Committee on the Judiciary, March 17, 2021 https://www.judiciary.senate.gov/meetings/the-equality-act-lgbtq-rights-are-human-rights, quoted by Joshua Pauling, "What Are Bodies For? Beyond Bathrooms and Women's Sports," *Public Discourse: The Journal of the Witherspoon Institute*, June 20, 2021, https://www.thepublicdiscourse.com/2021/06/76414/.

162   **some responses that will equip us to defend ourselves:** This content is adapted from a larger discussion in Jim Denison, *Between Compromise and Courage* (Dallas, Texas: Denison Forum, 2021), 5–30.

162   **"from 1500 to 1800":** Quoted by Jonah Goldberg, "American Passover: Juneteenth is a great American holiday," The Dispatch, June 18, 2021, https://gfile.thedispatch.com/p/american-passover.

164   **What the Bible says about racism:** For a more in-depth discussion of this topic, see chapter 1 in my book, *Between Compromise and Courage.*

169   **Old Scofield Reference Bible of 1909 interprets Genesis 9:24–25:** *The Old Scofield Study Bible King James Version, Classic Edition* (Oxford University Press).

169   **Dr. Tony Evans addresses this issue:** Tony Evans, "Are Black People Cursed? The Curse of Ham," Eternal Perspective Ministries, January 18, 2010, https://www.epm.org/resources/2010/Jan/18/are-black-people-cursed-curse-ham/.

169   **When oil wells were first dug:** For these and other examples, see John P. Newport and William Cannon, *Why Christians Fight Over the Bible* (Nashville, TN: Thomas Nelson, 1974).

Chapter 12: Defending biblical Christians with courage and hope

173   **"deadliest plants in North America":** Joe Boggs and Erik Draper, "Poison Hemlock and Wild Parsnip are going to Seed in Southern Ohio," Buckeye Yard & Garden online, June 21, 2019, https://bygl.osu.edu/node/1321.

173   **the spotted water hemlock:** Dan Nosqwitz, "Meet the Most Toxic Plant in North America," Atlas Obscura, December 14, 2017, https://www.atlasobscura.com/articles/spotted-water-hemlock-toxic-plant.

174   **the US has "transform[ed] the principle of non-establishment":** Harold O. J. Brown, *The Sensate Culture: Western Civilization Between Chaos and Transformation* (Dallas, TX: Word, 1996) 24.

175   **more than ten thousand distinct religions in the world:** Eds. George Thomas Kurian, David B. Barrett, Todd M. Johnson, *World Christian Encyclopedia: The world by segments: religions, peoples, languages, cities, topics* (United Kingdom: Oxford University Press, 2001).

176   **the deaths of more than sixty-two million babies:** Randall, O'Bannon, "62,502,904 Babies Have Been Killed in Abortions Since Roe v. Wade in 1973," LifeNews.com, January 18, 2021, https://www.lifenews.com/2021/01/18/62502904-babies-have-been-killed-in-abortions-since-roe-v-wade-in-1973/.

177   **"It is not religion that causes intolerance":** Keith Ward, *Is Religion Dangerous? New Edition* (United Kingdom: Lion Hudson Limited, 2011), 39, 56, 66.

177   **"no fewer than 20 million Soviet citizens were put to death"**: David Satter, "100 Years of Communism—and 100 Million Dead," *New York Times*, November 6, 2017, https://www.wsj.com/articles/100-years-of-communismand-100-million-dead-1510011810.

178   **"Freedom means you get to control the choice"**: Tony Evans, *How Should Christians Vote?* (Chicago, Illinois: Moody Press, 2012), 11–12.

178   **"It is said that after God died:"** Erwin W. Lutzer, *When a Nation Forgets God: 7 Lessons We Must Learn from Nazi Germany* (United States: Moody Publishers, 2015), 10.

179   **religious beliefs "give people a sense of meaning"**: Sally Quinn, "Religion is a sure route to true happiness," *The Washington Post*, 24 January 2014, https://www.washingtonpost.com/national/religion/religion-is-a-sure-route-to-true-happiness/2014/01/23/f6522120-8452-11e3-bbe5-6a2a3141e3a9_story.html.

179   **"people can live longer if they actively engage in formal religious activities"**: Philip Moeller, "Religion Makes People Happier—But Why?" *US News & World Report*, 12 April 2012, https://money.usnews.com/money/personal-finance/articles/2012/04/12/religion-makes-people-happierbut-why.

180   **"Of all the dispositions and habits which lead to political prosperity"**: George Washington, "Farewell Address," The Avalon Project, Yale Law School, http://avalon.law.yale.edu/18th_century/washing.asp.

180   **"our Constitution was made only for a moral and religious people"**: John Adams, "From John Adams to Massachusetts Militia, 11 October 1798," Founders Online, National Archives, https://founders.archives.gov/documents/Adams/99-02-02-3102

180   **"the general principles on which the fathers achieved independence"**: "John Adams to Thomas Jefferson, June 28, 1813" Founders Online, National Archives, https://founders.archives.gov/documents/Jefferson/03-06-02-0208.

180   **"Suppose a nation in some distant region"**: "Founding Father Quote #1282," Founding Father Quotes, https://www.foundingfatherquotes.com/quote/1282.

180   **"Injustice in government undermines the foundations of a society"**: "Moral Degeneracy," Thomas Jefferson on Politics & Government, http://107.6.21.207/Subjects/Politics/ThomasJefferson/jeff0250.htm.

180   **"It seems to me that nothing short of infinite wisdom"**: S. Trevena Jackson, *Lincoln's Use of the Bible* (New York: Abingdon Press, 1909), 14, https://www.gutenberg.org/files/38434/38434-h/38434-h.htm.

181   **"The church did preserve ancient classical culture"**: Keith Ward, *Is Religion Dangerous? New Edition* (United Kingdom: Lion Hudson Limited, 2011), 72.

181   **"Christians who did the most for the present world"**: C. S. Lewis, *Mere Christianity* (New York: Macmillan, 1977), 118.

182   **nine of the ten best nations on earth for women's rights:** John S. Dickerson, *Jesus Skeptic: A Journalist Explores the Credibility and Impact of Christianity* (Baker Books, 2019).

182   **"These great scientists who unlocked the Scientific Revolution"**: Dickerson, 29, 60, 71, 99, 110.

183   **one of the great historians of spiritual awakening:** J. Edwin Orr, "Prayer and Revival," Revival Library, https://www.revival-library.org/resources/revival_seekers/pray_for_revival/prayer_and_revival_orr.shtml.

184   **the evangelist famously regretted some of his political statements:** See, for instance, his statements in: Billy Graham, compiled by Collin Hansen, "What I Would Have Done Differently," *Christianity Today*, https://www.christianitytoday.com/ct/2018/billy-graham/what-i-would-have-done-differently.html.

185   **"If you asked today, 'What is an evangelical?' to most people"**: Rachel Martin, "'How Did We Get Here?' A Call For An Evangelical Reckoning On Trump," NPR, January 13, 2021, https://www.npr.org/sections/insurrection-at-the-capitol/2021/01/13/955801878/how-did-we-get-here-a-call-for-an-evangelical-reckoning-on-trump.

185   **"The connection between Christianity and the Republican Party"**: Matt Lewis, "The Evangelicals' Trump Obsession Has Tarnished Christianity," The Daily Beast, March 21, 2021, https://www.thedailybeast.com/the-evangelicals-trump-obsession-has-tarnished-christianity.

185   **"I came close to identifying the American way of life with the kingdom of God"**: Billy Graham, compiled by Collin Hansen, "What I Would Have Done Differently," *Christianity Today*, https://www.christianitytoday.com/ct/2018/billy-graham/what-i-would-have-done-differently.html.

187   **two million Christians were killed:** "Ancient Christian Martyrdom," Dallas Baptist University, https://www3.dbu.edu/mitchell/anceint_ christian_martyrdom.htm.

187   **"Our waking lives more and more resemble":** Chad Engelland, "Alexa, make me happy: Consumerism delivers temporary joy, but we need something deeper", https://edition.pagesuite.com/popovers/ dynamic_article_popover.aspx?artguid=4d68435d-2da2-4f64-acb5-0f9e4b6fc659&appid=3565.

188   **"Blessing those who have hurt you":** Craig Denison, "Bless Those Who Persecute You," First15, June 14, https://www.first15.org/06/14/ bless-those-who-persecute-you/.

189   **Christians have expansive religious freedoms:** For more, see Jim Denison, "What does the Bible say about religious liberty?" Denison Forum, August 3, 2020, https://www.denisonforum.org/resources/ what-does-the-bible-say-about-religious-liberty/.

190   **the blood of the martyrs:** The full quote is: "The oftener we are mown down by you, the more in number we grow; the blood of Christians is seed." Tertullian, *Apology*, Chapter 50, https://www.newadvent.org/ fathers/0301.htm.

190   **"There are things that can be seen only with eyes that have cried":** John L. Allen, Jr., *The Global War on Christians: Dispatches from the Front Lines of Anti-Christian Persecution*, (New York: Image, 2013), 49.

190   **"We who hated and destroyed one another":** Justin Martyr, "First Apology 14," *New Advent*, https://www.newadvent.org/fathers/0126. htm.

191   **"We love one another":** "The Octavius of Minucius Felix," *Ante-Nicene Fathers, Vol IV*, https://st-takla.org/books/en/ecf/004/0040034. html.

Conclusion: How to be the change we wish to see

193   **135 confirmed tsunamis . . . . distant tsunami sources:** "Hawaii Tsunamis," International Tsunami Information Center, http://itic.ioc-unesco.org/index.php?option=com content&view=category&layout=blog&id=1436&Itemid=1436.

194   **"We are living in the midst of a revolution":** R. Albert Mohler, Jr., *We Cannot Be Silent: Speaking Truth to a Culture Redefining*

Sex, Marriage, & the Very Meaning of Right & Wrong (Nashville, Tennessee: Nelson Books, 2015), 1.

194   **a way to stop tsunamis before they reach land:** David Nield, "A Mathematician Says He's Found a System That Could Stop Tsunamis in Their Tracks," ScienceAlert.com, January 27, 2017, https://www.sciencealert.com/scientists-have-a-plan-to-stop-tsunamis-with-sound-waves.

194   **adapted from Richard Niebuhr's classic book *Christ and Culture*:** H. Richard Niebuhr, *Christ & Culture* (New York: Harper & Row, 1951).

196   **we must do more than seek the "right to be wrong":** For an excellent expression of this fact, see Ryan T. Anderson, "Religious Liberty Isn't Enough," *The Wall Street Journal*, January 31, 2021, https://www.wsj.com/articles/religious-liberty-isnt-enough-11612125595.

197   **political without being partisan:** Ross Douthat, *Bad Religion: How We Became A Nation of Heretics* (New York: Free Press, 2012) 284–93.

197   **"It is not enough for Americans to respect orthodox Christianity":** Douthat, 293.

198   **"The great challenge of the Church today":** Phil Cooke, "How Christianity Lost Its Voice in Today's Media Driven World," HuffPost, 5 December 2012, https://www.huffpost.com/entry/how-christianity-lost-its-voice_b_2233928.

199   **"We are not here to attack or fight our neighbors":** John S. Dickerson, *Hope of Nations: Standing Strong in a Post Truth, Post-Christian World* (Grand Rapids, Michigan: Zondervan, 2018) 234.

199   **I encourage Christians to be people of civility:** Jim Denison, *Respectfully, I Disagree: How to Be a Civil Person in an Uncivil Time* (Dallas, Texas: Denison Forum, 2020), 39–87.

199   **culture changes "top down":** James Davison Hunter, *To Change the World: The Irony, Tragedy, and Possibility of Christianity in the Late Modern World* (New York: Oxford University Press, 2010). For more, see Jim Denison, "How to change the world," Denison Forum, July 23, 2011, https://www.denisonforum.org/columns/reviews/how-to-change-the-world/.

199   **Identify your spiritual gifts:** Jim Denison, "What are my spiritual gifts? An online spiritual gifts test," Denison Forum, https://www.denisonforum.org/spiritual-gifts-assessment/.

200   **"The place God calls you to":** Frederick Buechner, "Vocation," FrederickBuechner.com, June 18, 2017, https://www. frederickbuechner.com/quote-of-the-day/2017/7/18/vocation.

200   **"Love does not hoard itself up":** Anthony Esolen, *Out of the Ashes: Rebuilding American Culture* (Washington, DC: Regnery Publishing, 2017) 189.

201   **much that was unapologetically Christian:** Chris Armstrong, "When World Leaders Pray," *Christianity Today*, https://www. christianitytoday.com/history/2008/august/when-world-leaders-pray. html.

201   **"a woman of strong faith":** Quoted by Chris Armstrong, "When World Leaders Pray, Part II," *Christianity Today*, https://www. christianitytoday.com/history/2008/august/when-world-leaders-pray-part-ii.html.

202   **"American politics simply mirrors the loss of character":** Quoted in James Montgomery Boice, *Two Cities, Two Loves: Christian Responsibility in a Crumbling Culture* (Downers Grove, Illinois: InterVarsity Press, 1996) 27.

203   **when Chick-fil-A was targeted several years ago by LGBTQ activists:** Jim Denison, "Chick-fil-A and gay marriage," Denison Forum, July 25, 2012, https://www.denisonforum.org/columns/daily-article/chick-fil-a-and-gay-marriage/.

203   **many Christians have chosen no longer to shop at Target:** For more, see Ryan Denison, "Transgender person arrested for voyeurism at Target," Denison Forum, July 15, 2016, https://www.denisonforum.org/ columns/america/transgender-person-arrested-for-voyeurism-at-target/.

203   **civility is vital:** For more, see Jim Denison, *Respectfully, I Disagree: How to Be a Civil Person in an Uncivil Time* (Dallas, Texas: Denison Forum, 2020).

203   **"To be culturally literate is to":** E. D. Hirsch Jr., *Cultural Literacy: What Every American Needs to Know*, updated and expanded (New York: Vintage Books, 1988) xiii.

204   **Nations ascend due to the supremacy of their material resources:** Paul Kennedy, *The Rise and Fall of the Great Powers: Economic Change and Military Conflict from 1500 to 2000* (New York: Vintage Books, 1989).

204   **similarities between their empire and ours:** Cullen Murphy, *Are We Rome: The Fall of an Empire and the Fate of America* (Boston: Houghton Mifflin Company, 2007).

206   **"The strongest weapon in the world is sanctity. . . . If you will look into your own heart":** Peter Kreeft, *How to Win the Culture War: A Christian Battle Plan for a Society in Crisis* (Downers Grove, Illinois: InterVarsity Press, 2002) 100–3.

206   **Do you "wholly want to be"?:** For biblical ways to experience God's transforming presence every day, see Jim Denison, *Every Hour I Need Thee: A Practical Guide to Daily Prayer* (Dallas, Texas: Denison Forum, 2021).

206   **"We are neophiliacs":** Richard John Neuhaus, *The Naked Public Square: Religion and Democracy in America*, 2d ed. (Grand Rapids, Michigan: William B. Eerdmans Publishing Company, 1986 [1984]), 3.

207   **spoke out against the cultural sins of their day . . . . missionary to the Gentile world:** For more, see Jim Denison, *The State of Our Nation: 7 Critical Issues* (Dallas, Texas: Denison Forum, 2016), chapter 7.

207   **"A culture is unsalvageable if":** Jane Jacobs, *Dark Age Ahead* (New York: Random House, 2004) 24.

207   **"we shall be as a city upon a hill":** Quoted in Joel Rosenberg, *Implosion: Can America Recover From Its Economic & Spiritual Challenges in Time?* (Carol Stream, Illinois: Tyndale House Publishers, Inc., 2012) 319, 347.

208   **"By remaining faithful to its original commission":** Quoted by Russell Moore, *Onward: Engaging the Culture Without Losing the Gospel* (Nashville, Tennessee: B&H Publishing Group, 2015) vii.

208   **"no enemies, only opponents":** Quoted by Mitch Daniels, "February 11, 2011 Remarks, Ronald Reagan Centennial Dinner, Conservative Political Action Conference", http://www.p2012.org/photos11/cpac11/daniels021111sp.html.

208   **"It is important to get the idea of God right":** K. Randel Everett, *Pillars: The Ten Commandments . . . still standing after centuries of change* (Keller, TX: Austin Brothers Publishing, 2012), 19.

209   **"There still remains only God to protect man":** Quoted by Os Guinness, *Renaissance: The Power of the Gospel However Dark the Times* (United States: InterVarsity Press, 2014), 9.

210   **"Make we wise today"**: John Baillie, *A Diary of Private Prayer* (New York: Scribner), Kindle.

210   **"students were asked to choose sides in a classroom . . . . The day of casual Christianity is over"**: Erwin W. Lutzer, *Where Do We Go From Here? Hope and Direction in Our Present Crisis* (Chicago, Illinois: Moody Publishers, 2013), 13, 39.

211   **"Be of good comfort, Master Ridley"**: Richard Cavendish, "Latimer and Ridley Burned at the Stake," History Today, October 2005, https://www.historytoday.com/archive/latimer-and-ridley-burned-stake.

212   **"Mustard must be crushed"**: Shane Claiborne, *The Irresistible Revolution: Living as an Ordinary Radical* (Grand Rapids, Michigan: Zondervan, 2006), 337.

213   **"During the terrible Boxer Rebellion"**: Erwin W. Lutzer, *Where Do We Go From Here? Hope and Direction in Our Present Crisis* (Chicago, Illinois: Moody Publishers, 2013), 50.

213   **"we don't think anyone is beyond redemption"**: David Chidester, *Patters of Power: Religion & Politics in American Culture* (Englewood Cliffs, NJ: Prentice Hall, 1988), 293.

214   **"Can the Christian church in the advanced modern world"**: Os Guinness, *Renaissance: The Power of the Gospel However Dark the Times* (Downers Grove, Illinois: IVP Books, 2014), 14.

214   Christians **"should enjoy a worldwide boom"**: Philip Jenkins, *The Next Christendom: The Coming of Global Christianity* (New York: Oxford University Press, 2002), 2–3.

214   **the subject of religious commitment in America:** Glenn T. Stanton, *The Myth of the Dying Church: How Christianity Is Actually Thriving in America and the World* (New York: Worthy Publishing, 2019).

215   **the percentage of Americans who attend a local church:** For more, see Jim Denison, "Is the church nearly dead? Dr. Denison reviews 'The Myth of the Dying Church,'" Denison Forum, September 5, 2019, https://www.denisonforum.org/columns/book-reviews-excerpts/is-the-church-nearly-dead-dr-denison-reviews-the-myth-of-the-dying-church/.

216   **most popular hymn on the database:** "Most Popular Texts," Hymnary.org, https://hymnary.org/browse/popular/texts.